DATE DUE

GENES & DISEASE

TAY-SACHS DISEASE

GENES & DISEASE

GENES & DISEASE

TAY-SACHS
DISEASE

Jeri Freedman

CHELSEA HOUSE
PUBLISHERS
An imprint of Infobase Publishing

Tay-Sachs Disease

Copyright © 2009 by Infobase Publishing

All rights reserved. No part of this book may be reproduced or utilized in any form or by any means, electronic or mechanical, including photocopying, recording, or by any information storage or retrieval systems, without permission in writing from the publisher. For information contact:

Chelsea House
An imprint of Infobase Publishing
132 West 31st Street
New York NY 10001

Library of Congress Cataloging-in-Publication Data
Freedman, Jeri.
  Tay-Sachs disease / Jeri Freedman.
    p. cm.—(Genes and disease)
  Includes bibliographical references and index.
  ISBN 978-0-7910-9634-5 (hardcover)
  1. Tay-Sachs disease. I. Title. II. Series.
RJ399.T36F74 2009
618.92'858845—dc22   2008044770

Chelsea House books are available at special discounts when purchased in bulk quantities for businesses, associations, institutions, or sales promotions. Please call our Special Sales Department in New York at (212) 967–8800 or (800) 322–8755.

You can find Chelsea House on the World Wide Web at
http://www.chelseahouse.com

Text and design by Annie O'Donnell
Cover design by Ben Peterson

Printed in the United States of America

Bang NMSG 10 9 8 7 6 5 4 3 2 1

This book is printed on acid-free paper.

All links and Web addresses were checked and verified to be correct at the time of publication. Because of the dynamic nature of the Web, some addresses and links may have changed since publication and may no longer be valid.

CONTENTS

1

WHAT IS
TAY-SACHS DISEASE?

Leah was a beautiful, happy baby, and her parents were delighted when she was born. But before long, it became apparent that something was wrong. Her body seemed floppy, and even when she was several months old, she did not roll over as most babies do. Her parents were worried, but when they asked Leah's doctor about it, he said she was just developing a little slower than other children and would catch up. As time passed, Leah neither crawled nor tried to sit up. As she approached her first birthday, she started to have trouble swallowing food and breathing. Her parents rushed her to the hospital. Medical tests showed that her liver was abnormally large. An eye exam revealed cherry-colored spots on the back of her **retinas**—the layer of cells located in the back of the eye.

The combination of her symptoms and developmental delays led her doctor to suspect she might have a **metabolic disease** (a disease caused by the malfunctioning of processes in her body), so he referred her to a **geneticist**—an expert in diseases caused by defective genes. The geneticist performed blood tests, which revealed a lack of the enzyme hexosaminidase A. Leah had Tay-Sachs disease.

Tay-Sachs is a rare, hereditary disease in which the lack of an **enzyme**—a substance that controls a chemical reaction in the body—leads to a buildup of fats in nerve and brain cells. This causes the gradual destruction of nerves in the brain and body, leading to the loss of mental and physical abilities such as speech, movement, sight, and the ability to learn new skills. It eventually leads to death.

Tay-Sachs mostly affects Jews of Eastern European ancestry (known as **Ashkenazi** Jews). About 1 in 30 Ashkenazi Jews carry the Tay-Sachs gene worldwide. In comparison, about 1 in 280 people in the general population have the gene.

Children born with Tay-Sachs disease rarely live longer than five years from birth, although there is a rare (compared to other forms of the disease) **late-onset** form. It is called late onset because it occurs later in life—in adults rather than in children.

This chapter will explore the nature of genetic diseases in general and the biological processes that are specifically involved in Tay-Sachs disease.

WHAT IS TAY-SACHS DISEASE?

Tay-Sachs disease is a **hereditary disease**, meaning it is passed from parent to child. In most cases, Tay-Sachs disease affects babies. In typical cases, a baby appears normal from birth to about six months old. Around that time, affected children start to show a loss of muscle tone and problems with vision, swallowing, and breathing. The baby will often respond in an exaggerated way to sudden noises. Around two years of age, the child will start to have muscle **seizures** which are violent, uncontrollable muscle movements. In addition, children will experience problems with mental functioning and start to lose skills they had learned. Over time, they completely lose the ability to perform even basic activities such as crawling or sitting. In the end, the child becomes blind, paralyzed, and unresponsive, and ultimately dies, usually by five years of age.

WHAT ARE GENETIC DISEASES?

Tay-Sachs disease is also referred to as a **genetic disease**, which means it is an ailment that children inherit from their parents. Genetic diseases are caused by a mutation in one of the genes that tell the human body how to produce the substances that it needs to function. Genes are the basic elements of inheritance, and every person has 20,000 to 25,000 different genes. Genes control the production of substances called proteins, which, in turn, control bodily processes and make up body tissues. Most genes contain information in the form of a code that tells the body how to produce a particular protein. Some codes control how much protein is made or assist in making the proteins in other ways. For example, one gene may tell another gene to start producing growth hormone, and another gene may tell it to stop so that the body has just the right amount. Genetic diseases are caused by a defect in a gene. Tay-Sachs disease occurs because a defective gene prevents the production of certain enzyme called hexosaminidase A.

THE STRUCTURE OF GENES

Genetic information is encoded in the body by **deoxyribonucleic acid** (**DNA**). DNA carries genetic information in the form of a code made up of a pattern of four chemical bases: adenine (A), guanine (G), cytosine (C), and thymine (T). These bases bind, or link, to each other in pairs: A binds with T; C binds with G. Each of these pairs is called a *base pair*. Two other molecules—a sugar molecule and a phosphate molecule—bind to each base pair to form a

nucleotide. Two strands of nucleotides bind together, twist-
ing around each other to form a structure shaped like a
spiral staircase, with the base pairs forming the steps and

Double Helix

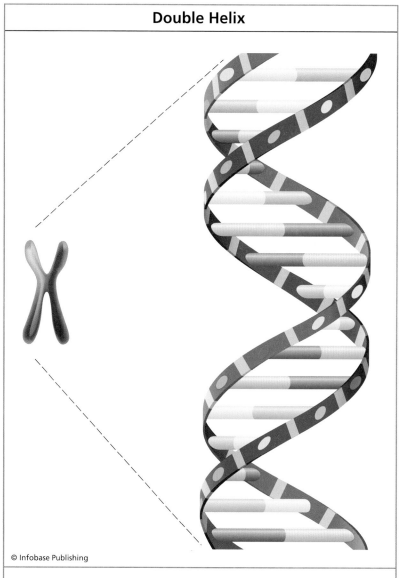

FIGURE 1.1 Chromosomes are made up of tightly wound bundles
of DNA and protein called chromatin.

the phosphate and sugar molecules providing the vertical sides that support the structure. This structure is called the double helix.

Most DNA in our bodies is found in the **chromosomes**, which are long, hair-like strands located in the nucleus, or center, of our cells. Human beings have 23 pairs of chromosomes, and one copy of each chromosome is inherited from each parent. The DNA in the chromosomes is divided into short sequences, called genes, each of which encodes a specific piece of genetic information.

HOW GENES FUNCTION

Genes for a particular **trait** can be either **dominant** or **recessive.** If a gene for a trait is *dominant*, then only one copy is necessary for a trait to manifest. For example, an individual who receives a gene for brown eyes from one parent and a gene for blue eyes from the other parent will have brown eyes because the gene for brown eyes is *dominant.* If a gene is *recessive*, then the trait it controls will only manifest if a person receives two copies of it, one from each parent. For instance, because blue eyes are a recessive trait, individuals with blue eyes must have received the gene for them from both parents.

Sometimes a person has one gene for a trait that is recessive and one gene for a trait that is dominant, as is the case in the eye color example discussed in the previous paragraph. For example, some women have one gene for color blindness that they received from their father and one normal gene from their mother. Therefore, they can see color normally. When a person does not have a disorder but has a gene for it that they can pass on, they are said to be **carriers** of the gene for that disorder. Thus, the women in the color blindness example who have one gene for color blindness are said to be carriers of that particular gene.

DISCOVERING THE DOUBLE HELIX

The structure of the DNA in our chromosomes was discovered by James Watson (1928–) and Frances Crick (1916–2004) in 1953. Chicago-born James Watson performed research at the Cavendish Laboratory in Cambridge, England, in the 1950s. There, a technique called X-ray diffraction was being used to study the molecular structure of various biological compounds. In X-ray diffraction, X-rays are bounced off a material, such as DNA. The resulting pattern is captured on the X-ray film, allowing scientists to see the arrangement of the molecules in the material being tested. At the same time that Watson was at Cambridge, Francis Crick, an English graduate student, was also at Cambridge, writing his dissertation on using X-ray crystallographic techniques to understand the structure of hemoglobin, a component of blood. Since Watson and Crick were both interested in the structure of DNA, they started working together. They tried building physical models of possible arrangements of the elements that make up DNA, working closely with two scientists at Cavendish: Maurice Wilkins (1916–2004) and Rosalind Franklin (1920–1958), experts in the then new field of X-ray diffraction. Using the X-ray diffraction data, Watson and Crick were able to deduce the structure of DNA and construct a three-dimensional model of the double helix, two strands that twisted around each other. Knowledge of the structure of DNA opened up vast new possibilities for the field of genetics, making it possible to identify specific genes, learn their function, identify which genes caused specific diseases, and develop ways of treating genetic diseases.

Although Franklin's research was used without her permission, it provided the basis for the work of Watson, Crick, and Wilkins, who were awarded the Nobel Prize for their work in 1962. Franklin died in 1958, so she could not receive the prize, which is only awarded to living researchers.

Tay-Sachs disease is a recessive genetic disease. In order for a baby to develop Tay-Sachs disease, it must receive a defective recessive gene from both parents. A person who inherits only one copy of the defective gene will not have the disease but will be a carrier.

HOW ARE GENES PASSED ON?

New cells are created in the body by cell division. In this process, an existing cell is copied to make a duplicate cell. There are two types of cell division. The first is called **mitosis**. In mitosis, all the contents of an existing, or parent, cell are duplicated, including all of the 46 chromosomes in the nucleus. The duplicate cells then split to form two new cells. This is how new body cells, such as skin cells, are created.

Sperm and egg cells are generated by a different type of cell division, called **meiosis**. In meiosis, 23 pairs of chromosomes are duplicated, but division takes place twice. The first division produces a pair of child cells, each of which has 23 pairs of chromosomes. Next, in each of those two cells, the 23 pairs of chromosomes separate into their individual chromosomes, which move to opposite sides of the cell. A second division takes place in which each daughter cell divides into two new cells, each with one set of 23 chromosomes. This process leads to a total of four cells, each with only 23 chromosomes. These are called **haploid** (Greek for "single") cells, because each has only half the number of chromosomes found in other body cells. This process ensures that when a sperm and egg cell combine, the result will be cells that include the correct number of chromosomes—46.

Meiosis is important because it allows for a mixing of chromosomes within a species. If every offspring had an exact duplicate of its mother's cells, for instance, all the

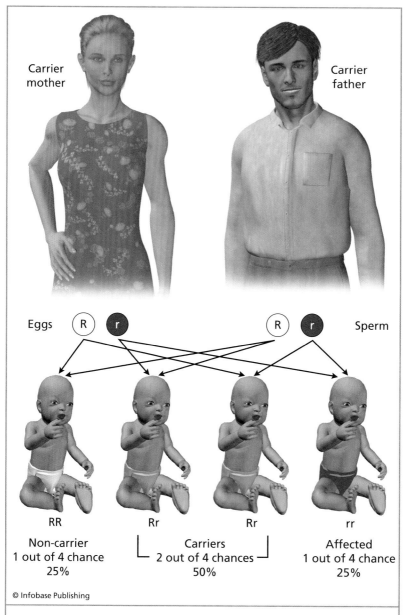

Eggs

Sperm

RR
Non-carrier
1 out of 4 chance
25%

Rr   Rr
⌐ Carriers ⌐
└ 2 out of 4 chances ┘
50%

rr
Affected
1 out of 4 chance
25%

© Infobase Publishing

FIGURE 1.2   In this drawing, the mother and father have one dominant and one recessive gene for Tay-Sachs disease. The four children illustrate the four different possible resulting combinations from this parent pair. As shown by the child on the far right, a child has a 1 out of 4 chance of having Tay-Sachs disease if both the mother and father are carriers of the gene.

mother's hereditary characteristics, including genetically-based problems, would be passed on to the child. Combining chromosomes from two sources is an advantage for two reasons: (1) It provides an opportunity for the offspring to get a "good" gene from one parent that compensates for a defective version from the other parent, and (2) It increases the chance that new combinations of traits will appear in offspring that enhance a species' ability to survive (for example, if a ginger cat with a gene for stripes mates with a solid gray cat, the resulting kittens may be gray with stripes instead of solid gray; therefore, they will be better camouflaged when surrounded by foliage, which will make it harder for predators to find them and helps ensure the cats' survival). It is the first aspect that is of interest when dealing with a disease like Tay-Sachs. As will be discussed in Chapter 2, the lack of genetic variance within a population can be a factor in the spread of a disease like Tay-Sachs.

HOW DO GENETIC MUTATIONS LEAD TO DISEASE?

The genes in the chromosomes are copied whenever a new cell is generated. A mutation is a change in the sequence of DNA that makes up a gene. Two causes of mutations include (1) random errors that occur when the chromosome is being copied for inclusion in a new cell, and (2) direct damage to the chromosome (for example, through exposure to toxic chemicals or radiation). If the mutation takes place when a **somatic** (body) cell is being duplicated, then it can lead to a disease, such as **cancer** (which refers to cells of a given type that grow out of control).

If the mutation takes place when a sperm or egg cell is being produced, the change can be passed on to the child. This type of mutation is called a **germline mutation**. Once

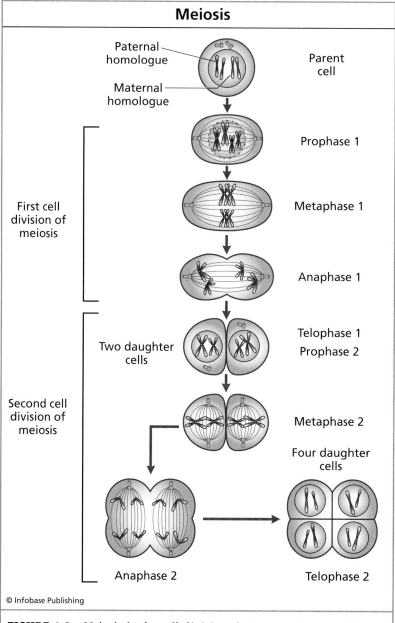

Meiosis

Paternal homologue

Maternal homologue

Parent cell

Prophase 1

Metaphase 1

Anaphase 1

First cell division of meiosis

Telophase 1
Prophase 2

Two daughter cells

Metaphase 2

Second cell division of meiosis

Four daughter cells

Anaphase 2

Telophase 2

© Infobase Publishing

FIGURE 1.3   Meiosis is the cell division that generates sex cells. Unlike mitosis, meiosis results in four daughter cells instead of two.

the mutation has occurred, if the sperm or egg cell that contains the defective gene becomes an embryo, that damaged gene will exist in the baby. Because all the cells in an individual's body have the exact copies of the same chromosomes, even individuals with defective genes who do not get sick with the disease may still pass that defective gene on to their offspring through their sperm or egg cells.

Every cell in the body depends on thousands of different proteins to function properly. All the tissues and compounds, such as the enzymes and hormones, that compose a body are made up of proteins. If a mutation causes one of these proteins to function incorrectly or not to be made at all, then this can affect the health or development of the body. When this happens, the resulting problem is called a **genetic disorder**. Many mutations that occur have no effect, either because they occur on genes that code recessive traits or because they do not affect an essential bodily process. When a mutation occurs that affects an important bodily process, however, the effects can be devastating.

WHAT ARE LIPID STORAGE DISORDERS?

In Tay-Sachs disease, the defective gene is responsible for producing an enzyme necessary to break down a **lipid**, a fatty substance produced in the body. Failure to produce this enzyme results in a type of disease called a **lipid storage disorder** because too much of this fat is stored in the cells, which causes harmful effects. Over time, this fat accumulates to the point where it damages body cells and tissues.

Tay-Sachs disease is a type of lipid storage disorder called a **lysosomal storage disease**. Most cells in the body contain **lysosomes**, which are one type of tiny organ-like

structures that are called *organelles*. Lysosomes are responsible for digesting, or breaking down, substances in the cell
that are no longer necessary. Lysosomes contain enzymes
that perform this digestion. There are 49 different lysosomal
storage diseases. They are all inherited, and all result from
the lack of one of the enzymes that lysosomes use to break
down material in the cell. When an enzyme necessary for
breaking down material is missing, the lysosomes fill up with
that material, ultimately swelling and damaging the cell. In
Tay-Sachs disease, the enzyme that breaks down a specific
type of lipid is absent; the result is that lipid fails to break

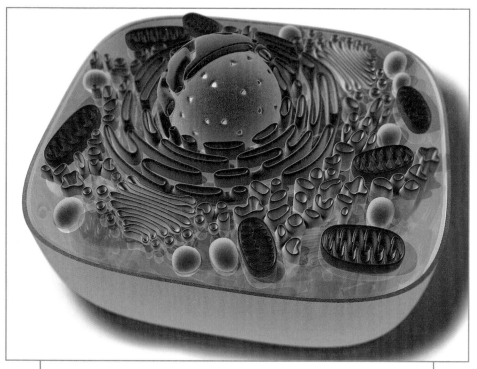

FIGURE 1.4 The lysosomes are the round, bright green structures
in this illustration of an animal cell. Other organelles, including the
nucleus, endoplasmic reticulum, mitochondria, and golgi apparatus,
are also visible.

down and fills up the lysosomes, ultimately destroying the cell. When too many of an organ's cells are destroyed, that organ stops functioning.

HOW DOES TAY-SACHS DISEASE OCCUR?

The specific lipid that is involved in Tay-Sachs disease is GM2 **ganglioside**, which is found in the brain. The term *ganglioside* was coined by German scientist Ernst Klenk in 1921 to describe a lipid he found in nerve cells called **ganglions**, which are nerve cells located at the base of the brain. Gangliosides are necessary for brain and nerve cells to develop properly.

Nerve cells in the brain, which are also called **neurons**, are insulated and protected by a sheath of white, fatty material called **myelin**. GM2 ganglioside binds to other molecules in the myelin sheath and is important in keeping it stable. The *myelin sheath* is important: Without this insulation, the signals sent and received by the nerve cells would interfere with each other, like static on a noisy telephone line or a badly tuned radio. If too much GM2 ganglioside builds up in the brain, it can result in damaged brain cells. Therefore, our bodies produce an enzyme called hexosaminidase A, often referred to as hex A, which breaks down GM2 ganglioside. Because of a defect in the HEXA gene, babies with Tay-Sachs disease do not produce the hex A enzyme. Therefore, GM2 ganglioside builds up in their brains, damaging and ultimately destroying brain cells, resulting in impaired function.

WHO WERE TAY AND SACHS?

Warren Tay (1843–1927) was a British **ophthalmologist** (a doctor who specializes in eye diseases). Tay studied medicine at London Hospital, where he qualified as a physician in

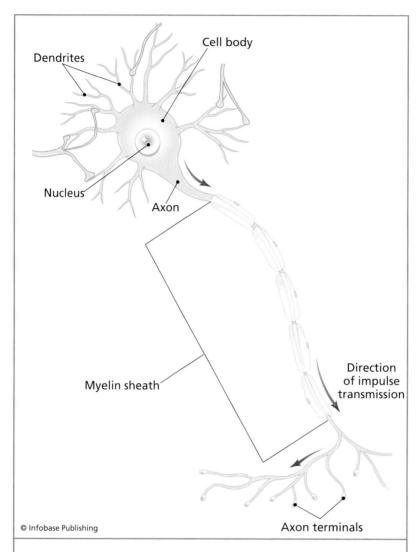

Dendrites

Cell body

Nucleus

Axon

Myelin sheath

Direction
of impulse
transmission

Axon terminals

© Infobase Publishing

FIGURE 1.5   The insulation that the myelin sheath—a layer of soft, fatty material covering the axon—gives neurons is important because it prevents signals sent and received by nerve cells from interfering with each other. The enzyme hexosaminidase A breaks down GM2 ganglioside, which helps keep the myelin sheath stable. Babies with Tay-Sachs do not produce hexosaminidase A, and their brain cells are destroyed when too much GM2 ganglioside builds up in the nerve cells.

1866. From 1868 to 1907, he was an assistant surgeon at the Hospital for Skin Disease at Blackfriars in England. In 1869, Tay also became an assistant surgeon and ophthalmologist at London Hospital, and later a senior surgeon. He was a founding member of the Ophthalmological Society. In an article in the first volume of the society's journal, he described distinctive spots that were present on the retina in a baby with **neurological** problems whom he had treated in 1881. This was the first description of the cherry-red dots on the back of the eye characteristic of the disease that would become known as Tay-Sachs disease. In 1894, in the fourth volume of the society's journal, he went on to give a complete description of the symptoms of the disease. He also observed that another member of the baby's family had the same retinal problem—a sign that the disease could run in families.

Bernard Sachs (1858–1944) was a prominent American **neurologist**, a doctor who specializes in diseases of the brain and nerves. The son of German-Jewish parents who had emigrated to New York, Sachs graduated with a bachelor's degree from Harvard Medical College in 1878 and went on to get a graduate degree from the University of Vienna in Austria in 1882. He stayed on to do postgraduate work on the anatomy of the brain and neurological disorders. In 1884, he returned to New York and went into private practice. In 1887, he started teaching at the New York Polyclinic Hospital. During this period, he wrote an article in which he, like Tay, described the cherry-red spots seen in the retina of infants suffering a neurological condition he named "amaurotic familial idiocy" (a term that is no longer used). He described the hereditary nature of Tay-Sachs disease and was the first to describe the changes that take place in cells affected by it. He went on to become a consultant at the Mount Sinai and

Manhattan State Hospitals, as well as becoming publisher of the *Journal of Nervous and Mental Disease* from 1886 to 1911 and president of the American Neurological Association from 1894 to 1932.

The two doctors were initially unaware of each other's work. However, it was eventually recognized that Tay and Sachs were describing the same disease—and so it became known as Tay-Sachs disease.

2

THE DEMOGRAPHICS OF TAY-SACHS

*D*emographics is a term that refers to the typical characteristics of a certain population. This chapter looks at the population that most commonly develops Tay-Sachs disease and the reasons why this group is affected.

WHO DEVELOPS TAY-SACHS DISEASE?

Tay-Sachs disease occurs worldwide in people of all ethnic backgrounds and religions. Historically, Tay-Sachs disease has occurred most commonly in people of Ashkenazi Jewish ancestry, but now it is also prevalent in non-Jewish populations, including people of French-Canadian/Cajun heritage. About 1 out of every 360,000 people in the general population gets Tay-Sachs disease compared to 1 out of every 3,600 people of Ashkenazi Jewish ancestry. While approximately 1 out of every 30 people of Ashkenazi Jewish ancestry carries the gene for Tay-Sachs, they do not develop the disease.

WHO ARE THE ASHKENAZI JEWS?

Ashkenazi (pronounced Ahsh-ke-nah-zi) Jews means "the Jews of the Ashenaz." Ashenaz was the Hebrew name for

FIGURE 2.1   Ashkenazi Jews pose in an 1876 image, taken in Jerusalem.

Germany in the Middle Ages. Ashkenazi Jews are the descendants of the Jews who lived in communities along the Rhine River in Germany at that time. They migrated there from the Middle East between A.D. 800 and 1000. Between the tenth and nineteenth centuries, they emigrated from Germany into Poland, Russia, and Eastern Europe. Later, mostly in the nineteenth century, many Ashkenazi Jews came to the United States to seek a better way of life, like so many other immigrants did at that time.

The **Yiddish** language evolved as the common language among Ashkenazi Jews. It developed from a combination of German, Hebrew, and **Aramaic** (an ancient language spoken in Syria, Palestine, and Mesopotamia). The majority of Jewish people living in America today are Ashkenazi Jews descended from European Jews. In fact, about 80% of Jews in the world today are Ashkenazi Jews. The remainder are those Jews who come from or live in the Middle East, as well as Jews whose ancestors lived in Spain and Portugal. They are called Sephardic Jews.

GENETIC MAKEUP OF ASHKENAZI JEWS

There are many ways to define a population such as Ashkenazi Jews. This can be done on the basis of a common culture, a shared religion, or a genetic identity. As far as the transmission of disease is concerned, it is the last method that is most important for our discussion. Beginning in the 1990s, after recognizing the increased occurrence of this disease among this population, researchers started to analyze the DNA of Ashkenazi Jews in order to find out where they originated. This information was important to understanding why Tay-Sachs disease is much more common among that population than in the general population. Such information also provides valuable insight into how genetic diseases spread within a population.

Researchers studied DNA that was unique to males or females among the Ashkenazi Jewish population. By studying both male and female DNA, scientists could trace the origin of genes that had been passed down through generations of Ashkenazi Jews. This information would allow researchers to identify whether the gene for Tay-Sachs originated in the Middle East, or whether it was introduced from Europeans with whom the Ashkenazi Jews mated. If it turned out that the Ashkenazi Jews had little in common genetically with the Europeans among whom they lived, this would support the idea that isolation from the larger population played a role in the prevalence of the disease within the Ashkenazi Jewish population.

In 2000, an international team of researchers, led by M.F. Hammer of the University of Arizona, Tucson, traced the **paternal** (male) origins of the Ashkenazi Jews. They used a set of genes found on the Y chromosome.

The Y chromosome determines that a child will be male. Every person has two chromosomes that determine their sex. A girl has two X chromosomes, one from her mother and one from her father. A boy has one X chromosome from his mother and one Y chromosome from his father. Since only boys have a Y chromosome, tracing the genes on this chromosome allows researchers to identify paternal ancestors.

Dr. Hammer's team of researchers examined the DNA of men from 29 populations, 7 of them Jewish (Ashkenazi, Roman, North African, Kurdish, Near Eastern, Yemenite, and Ethiopian) and 16 non-Jewish groups from similar geographic locations. The researchers were looking for specific **alleles**.

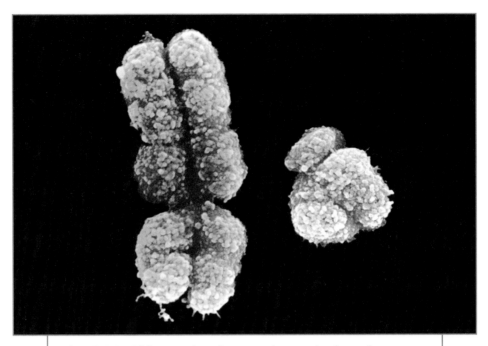

FIGURE 2.2   This scanning electron micrograph of sex chromosomes shows the X and Y chromosomes. Each chromosome has replicated, forming and joining with an identical copy, or chromatid.

An allele is a gene that codes for a particular variant of a trait like eye color. For example, the form of the gene for blue eye color and the form of the gene for brown eye color are different alleles.

A series of analyses was performed to find out whether the specific alleles, or varieties, of the genes on the Y chromosome of Ashkenazi Jewish men came mainly from a Middle Eastern population or from this population that interbred with the native non-Jewish populations in Europe. The analysis revealed only a few alleles in common with European populations. Instead, the study showed that the shared genes were the same as those in Middle Eastern non-Jewish populations, including Palestinians and Syrians. In other words, the Ashkenazi Jewish and Middle Eastern non-Jewish populations had the same genes on the Y-chromosome. The results supported the idea that the paternal gene pools of Jewish communities from Europe, North Africa, and the Middle East came from a common Middle Eastern source. This suggested that most Jewish communities remained isolated from neighboring non-Jewish communities in Europe. Dr. Hammer's research suggests that as Ashkenazi Jews migrated deeper into Europe from the Middle East through Italy and into Germany, these inhabitants encountered a series of **population bottlenecks** (events that reduce the size of a population). Such population shrinkage reduces the size of a given **gene pool** (the different genes that are available to be passed on to descendants).

Other team members studied **mitochondrial DNA**, which allows them to trace a gene back through generations to its original source. Mitochondrial DNA is found only in **mitochondria**, tiny organs located in our cells that are involved in the process of breaking down nutrients in the cell to produce energy. This type of DNA is passed on only from females because when the male's sperm fertilizes the female's egg, the sperm's mitochondria are discarded and the egg's mitochondria are passed on to all the child's cells when the fertilized egg cell divides.

In 2006, Doron M. Behar and Karl Skorecki of the Technion and Ramban Medical Center in Haifa, Israel, along with colleagues in numerous countries, simultaneously performed a study in which they analyzed the mitochondrial DNA of Ashkenazi Jews. They used complete sequences of DNA to trace their ancestry down the female line and found that 40% of present-day Ashkenazi Jews are descended from just four women. The study states, "Here, using complete sequences of maternally inherited mitochondrial DNA (mtDNA), we show that close to one-half of Ashkenazi Jews, estimated at 8,000,000 people, can be traced back to only four women carrying distinct mtDNAs that are virtually absent in other populations, with the important exception of low frequencies among non-Ashkenazi Jews. We conclude that four founding mtDNAs, likely of Near Eastern ancestry, underwent major expansion(s) in Europe within the past millennium." The study indicates that the women were also of Middle Eastern origin, providing further evidence that the allele for Tay-Sachs originated in the population of Jews that migrated from the Middle East to Europe. More importantly, however, the study indicates that a large portion of the Ashkenazi population is descended from this very small number of "founders" on the female side.

WHY DO CERTAIN POPULATIONS DEVELOP TAY-SACHS?

Scientists believe that the first Tay-Sachs mutation occurred about 1,000 years ago. There is some evidence, although it is controversial, that carriers of the Tay-Sachs mutation have a greater resistance to **tuberculosis**. Thus, the mutation may have provided protection from the **epidemics** of tuberculosis that swept through the crowded communities of Europe in the Middle Ages. This would have been a good thing—unless you inherited two copies of the defective gene, and thus developed Tay-Sachs disease. This raises the issues of **genetic drift** and the **founder effect**. These factors result in an increased prevalence of this genetic mutation among a particular population.

Genetic Drift

Genetic drift is the tendency of an inherited trait to become more or less common as it moves through generations of people. As previously mentioned, a given form of a gene is called an allele. There are two basic forces that affect the chance of an allele's occurrence in a given population. On one hand, there is natural selection. This is the tendency to build up alleles that provide a benefit that increases a population's chance of survival. Such alleles tend to become more common in a particular population because those who possess them live longer and, in theory, produce more offspring. Thus, the allele spreads throughout that population.

There is a second way in which an allele can become common, and this is through chance. This has proven to be true because events not related to natural selection can affect the survival of members of a given population. For example, if war or natural disaster destroys all but a small number of people, then the survivors' alleles will live on. Other alleles that were present in the part of the population that died do not survive and are not passed on to future generations. Whatever alleles the survivors possess will be passed throughout the remaining population, regardless of whether those alleles are good or bad, because they are the only ones that exist in that remaining population.

This is an important feature of genetic drift. The survival of the best alleles and the dying out of the least beneficial alleles depends on a population having a large number of people. If there is a large population and everyone in the population faces the same environmental challenges, then more of those with the "best" alleles will survive, and more of those with the "worst" alleles will die out. Under these circumstances, better alleles will spread throughout the population, and worse ones will become increasingly rare. This occurs because the better allele will be passed on by more people, and there will be fewer people to pass on the worse allele. The number of people who have the better allele increases, and the number of people with the worse allele decreases. Eventually, the better allele will be present in the majority of the people, and the worse allele will be present in very few people.

In small populations, however, this process does not necessarily work. A random mutation can spread rapidly throughout all or most members of the community. If there are only a small number of people in a community and they intermarry generation after generation, eventually a mutation can spread to the majority of the population.

This is true because genetic drift is basically a statistical phenomenon, and in statistics an effect is only evident in large numbers. For example, everyone knows that if you flip a coin, half the time it will come up heads and half the time it will come up tails. However, if you flip a coin 10 times, you might get 7 tails and 3 heads. If you make 1,000 tosses, you would see more equal amounts of heads and tails. The more tosses you make, the more likely that the end result will approach 50–50.

In large populations, natural selection tends to be the force that determines whether an allele survives. In a small population, genetic drift tends to **predominate**. If enough people in a certain population intermarry and pass the allele on to offspring who have one "good" gene and one "bad" gene, carriers of the "bad" allele can come to predominate the population. Such non-beneficial genetic drift is sometimes seen in small populations of people who have migrated to a new area where they are isolated from the majority of the population. This leads to a phenomenon called the *founder effect*.

The Founder Effect

The founder effect is a concept that was described in 1963 by evolutionary biologist Ernst Mayr (1904–2005). It is the creation of a new population started by a few founders who carry only a small subset of the gene pool of the original population. Mayr proposed that new species form when small populations of individuals who possess only a small subset of the original species' genes become isolated. Both the alleles that are possessed by the small **subpopulation** and any genetic mutations that occur rapidly spread throughout the group. Thus, the isolated group starts to vary from its parent population, and this variation can lead to the development of a new species. In human beings, however, it often leads to what scientists refer to as a *population bottleneck*.

In a population bottleneck, a subset of genetic traits from the parent population becomes common in the subpopulation. For example, if 50% of a population has trait A and 50% has trait B and a small number of people from this population sets out to settle in a remote area, it may consist of:

- 50% trait A and 50% trait B people
- mostly people who have trait A
- or mostly people with trait B

The children of the people in the second case are more likely to have trait A than trait B because trait A is more common in the population. In the third case, the children will be more likely to have trait B because it is more common in that population. **Inbreeding** among the small number of individuals will rapidly spread a gene throughout the population. When a mutation to a gene occurs in such a population, it is likewise spread throughout the population, creating a founder effect. This is one reason that both Ashkenazi Jews and other founder populations (see the sidebar) have high rates of Tay-Sachs disease.

TAY-SACHS IN OTHER FOUNDER POPULATIONS

The Jewish population is not the only one to suffer from Tay-Sachs disease. French-Canadian populations in southern and eastern Quebec and their descendants, the Cajuns in Louisiana, also suffer from Tay-Sachs disease. Approximately 1 in 30 French Canadians and Cajuns are carriers of a Tay-Sachs mutation. The genetic defect that most commonly causes Tay-Sachs in the French-Canadian population in Quebec has been traced back to a family that lived in southern Quebec in the 1680s.

Approximately 1 in 50 Irish Americans carry a Tay-Sachs mutation. Irish people, especially Catholics who immigrated to America, were often forced to live in their own communities separate from the mainstream English and Protestant populations. In this way, their situation was similar to that of Ashkenazi Jews. Tay-Sachs disease also occurs at a higher-than-normal rate among Amish communities in America. This population is a religious sect descended from the followers of a Swiss bishop named Jakob Ammann. They came to the United States in the seventeenth century and settled in Pennsylvania, Ohio, and Indiana as well as parts of Canada. From that time until the twentieth century they kept themselves separate from the mainstream population, following their own religious and social customs.

All these groups developed from small populations that were socially isolated from the mainstream populations. Over time, marriages within these small communities allowed the genetic mutations that cause the disease to spread among a large number of people in the group.

These populations all have unusually high levels of Tay-Sachs disease, and in each case, the disease is caused by a mutation

(continues)

(continued)

of the gene responsible for generating the enzyme hexosaminidase A, commonly called hex A. However, the exact mutation that causes the disease is different in the various populations. This is an example of how one disease can be caused by more than one type of mutation in a gene. In this case, even though the changes to the gene are different, the end result is the same—the gene does not work the way it should. As a result, the enzyme hex A is not produced and lipid builds up in the brain cells, causing irreversible damage.

FIGURE 2.3 This photo shows an Amish family riding an open buggy to town, as is the custom according to Amish practice of avoiding certain modern conveniences. Amish communities are another example of an isolated group that has been prone to Tay-Sachs disease.

MUTATIONS AND THE FOUNDER EFFECT

Currently, over a hundred different mutations have been identified that could cause Tay-Sachs disease. These various mutations have been found in different people worldwide. The significance of the founder effect, however, is that rather than appearing randomly in the general population, a mutation is passed on to subsequent generations of a small community that intermarries. In this way, what started out as a random mutation spreads to a large number of the people in the community. Thus, when scientists test members of the community, they find that a particular mutation is common in that group.

In the case of Ashkenazi Jews, two common mutations have been identified that cause the disease in infants. In one mutation, part of the gene is missing. This single mutation is responsible for 80% of the cases of Tay-Sachs that occur in the Ashkenazi Jewish population. In the other mutation, material at the end of the gene is deleted, rendering it inactive.

TYPES OF TAY-SACHS DISEASE

Tay-Sachs disease occurs in several different forms. While most cases of Tay-Sachs occur in infants and young children, there is an even rarer form that occurs later in life. This is called **late-onset Tay-Sachs.** All forms of Tay-Sachs disease are the result of a defect in the gene that produces the hexosaminidase A (hex A) enzyme. However, there are many different types of defects that can occur in this gene. Although the end result is the same, the cause is different. This chapter explains the different types of Tay-Sachs disease and describes a disease closely related to Tay-Sachs disease, called Sandhoff disease.

HOW HEXOSAMINIDASE A WORKS

In order to understand what causes Tay-Sachs disease, it is helpful to know how the hex A enzyme works. The hex A enzyme breaks down GM2 ganglioside through a process called **hydrolysis**. Hydrolysis is a word for using water to split something apart (*hydro* is Greek for "water"; *lysis* is Greek for "loosen" or "dissolve").

Dissolving GM2 ganglioside in the body requires the presence of three proteins that control the process of breaking it down. One of the proteins is an **activator protein**. An activator protein works with the enzyme hex A to cause the reaction to occur. The other two proteins are subunits or specific parts of the hex A enzyme. The hex A enzyme has two parts, called the *alpha subunit* and the *beta subunit*. *Alpha* and *beta* are Greek for the letters A and B. Thus, these

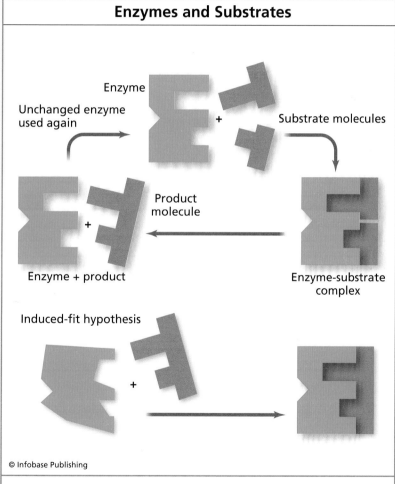

Enzymes and Substrates

Enzyme

Unchanged enzyme used again

Substrate molecules

Product molecule

Enzyme + product

Enzyme-substrate complex

Induced-fit hypothesis

© Infobase Publishing

FIGURE 3.1 An enzyme binds to a substrate (a molecule upon which an enzyme acts). Since each enzyme typically only works with a specific substrate or substrates in a specific reaction, this process is often described as resembling a lock and key system.

subunits are "part A" and "part B." If a person lacks any of these three proteins, the GM2 ganglioside cannot be broken up. When part of the gene that makes one of the subunits of the required hex A is defective, that subunit is either not produced at all or is not produced correctly. In that case, the GM2 ganglioside cannot be dissolved, and it builds up in nerve cells in the brain.

INFANTILE TAY-SACHS

Until he was six months old, Colin appeared to be a normal, healthy baby. He learned to roll over and sit up and had started to babble, squeal, and laugh. When Colin reached six months old, however, he started to have trouble with previously learned skills, and eventually he stopped performing them at all. He stopped making eye contact and started to experience seizures. By the time he was a year and a half old, he was almost totally paralyzed and blind. He could no longer eat on his own or drink out of a bottle, so he had to be fed with a feeding tube. He also needed oxygen from a tank to help him breathe. A few months later, Colin died.

The type of Tay-Sachs disease that occurs in babies is called *infantile Tay-Sachs*. It is also called **acute** infantile hexosaminidase A deficiency. (Doctors use the term "acute" to describe diseases that occur over a short period of time and have very strong symptoms.) Infantile Tay-Sachs is by far the most common type of Tay-Sachs disease. Of the approximately 100 types of mutations that occur on the HEXA gene—the gene for the enzyme hexosaminidase A—and cause Tay-Sachs disease, 90 of them result in infantile Tay-Sachs disease.

The affected babies appear totally normal when they are born. The first symptoms appear when the child is between three and six months old and they start to show signs of mild muscle weakness. The symptoms quickly worsen. Some jerking of the muscles also occurs, and the babies have a much stronger-than-normal startle response to sudden loud noises. (A startle response is the involuntary, or automatic, flexing of the muscles that occurs when a person is startled by a sudden sharp noise.)

From six to ten months of age, the baby fails to develop new **motor skills**. (Motor skills are those that rely on muscle control, such as crawling and walking.) The baby may also show a decrease in visual attention and make rapid involuntary eye movements. Babies with Tay-Sachs may even lose the muscle skills that they previously developed. Their vision becomes increasingly impaired and, eventually, the child goes blind. The retina (the reflective area at the back of the eye) becomes pale and a cherry-red spot appears on it. This is one of the most obvious signs of Tay-Sachs disease. The disease quickly gets worse after the baby is 10 months old; eventually the child becomes blind and paralyzed. Children with infantile Tay-Sachs usually live for two to four years from birth.

In children with infantile Tay-Sachs, the gene responsible for the production of the hex A enzyme is defective on both copies of chromosome 15—the one received from the child's mother and the one received from the child's father. Therefore, the child does not produce any hex A at all. One reason that the infantile form of Tay-Sachs causes such a rapid decline is that the complete lack of hex A leads to a large buildup of a type of *lipid*, or fat—the GM2 ganglioside—throughout the brain. In addition to the typical type of infantile Tay-Sachs disease, there is a very rare form of the disease in which the gene for hex A is normal and the child produces normal amounts of hex A. In this case, a different gene is defective—one that is responsible for producing another protein that breaks down the GM2

FIGURE 3.2 This six-year-old child is in the late stages of infantile Tay-Sachs disease, which has left her almost completely paralyzed. Many infants and children with Tay-Sachs disease are not expected to live beyond the first few years of life, as symptoms worsen with age.

ganglioside. The symptoms and course of this type of Tay-Sachs are identical to those of the more common type of Tay-Sachs.

JUVENILE TAY-SACHS

Jenny had been a perfectly normal infant and toddler. She was excited to start school, and liked playing soccer. Then things started to change. She started to stutter when she spoke and became increasingly clumsy and uncoordinated. Her parents, Gina and Henry, were worried and took her to the doctor. But the doctor could not find anything wrong. Frustrated, her parents consulted a geneticist. He identified her problem as juvenile Tay-Sachs disease.

Her parents did everything possible to keep her comfortable and happy. Eventually, Jenny's muscles became too weak for her to walk and she stopped talking. She had trouble eating and sometimes inhaled food into her lungs. Finally, taking care of her at home became too difficult and her parents had to take her to a **hospice,** a facility that takes care of people with terminal illnesses. They visit her frequently, and although she can not talk, she always gives them a smile.

Juvenile Tay-Sachs disease strikes children between the ages of 2 and 10 years old. This type of Tay-Sachs disease is also called juvenile (**subacute**) hexosaminidase A deficiency. The term *subacute* is used by doctors to describe a disease in which the symptoms take longer to appear, are not as severe as in an acute disease, and last for a longer period of time. In juvenile Tay-Sachs disease, symptoms usually appear between 2 and 10 years of age. The first signs are problems with muscle coordination, resulting in clumsiness and unsteadiness when walking, followed by problems with speech and comprehension. The child eventually develops seizures. However, problems with vision happen much later than in infantile Tay-Sachs, and the cherry-red spot does not always appear in the eye. The symptoms gradually become worse. Eventually, between 10 and 15 years old, the child becomes completely unresponsive. Death usually occurs within a few years, most commonly as the result of infection, because the child's immobility makes him or her susceptible to many types of infections, including frequent bouts of pneumonia.

LATE-ONSET TAY-SACHS

As a teenager, Frank stuttered and his speech was slurred. He was sent to a speech therapist, but despite his diligent efforts, his speech problems continued. He was slow and awkward at sports and was often the kid picked last for any team. He consoled himself with the thought that he did very well academically. He graduated from high school and college. He got a job as a computer programmer where his contact with other people was limited, so he did not have to worry about his speech problem.

As he got older, his coordination continued to get worse, his muscles got weaker, and he had frequent cramps in his limbs. He started to stumble when walking, and sometimes fell. He often had *tremors* (shaking) in his hands, which made it difficult to use a computer. Eventually, his coordination became so bad, he was forced to stop working and had to rely on disability insurance to pay his living expenses.

One day, he got a call from his sister. She told him that she and her husband had genetic testing done to see if they had any hereditary diseases they might pass on to their children. It turned out that she was a carrier of a genetic mutation that was linked to Tay-Sachs disease. She suggested that Frank get tested to see if he had any such genetic mutation that might be contributing to his problems. Frank had the test performed and discovered that he did indeed have a form of Tay-Sachs disease—late-onset Tay-Sachs disease (LOTS).

Although most cases of Tay-Sachs occur in infants and children, there is a late-onset form of the disease. This form of Tay-Sachs occurs in adults in their twenties and thirties. Because its symptoms are the same as a number of other neurological diseases and because Tay-Sachs is associated mostly with children, late-onset Tay-Sachs is often misdiagnosed. It is caused by different genetic mutations than those that cause Tay-Sachs in babies. Late-onset Tay-Sachs was identified in the 1970s as a result of routine screening of individuals who were potential carriers of the Tay-Sachs gene.

Most forms of late-onset Tay-Sachs disease progress slowly. In many cases, people with late-onset Tay-Sachs disease have some hex A enzyme, but very low levels. Because the amount of hex A produced by people with late-onset Tay-Sachs disease varies, so do the symptoms. In general, late-onset Tay-Sachs progresses more slowly than infantile and juvenile Tay-Sachs disease. However, it can still affect the muscles and mental functions.

The first symptoms of late-onset Tay-Sachs disease are muscle atrophy (shrinking), tremors, weakness, slurred speech, difficulty swallowing, and unsteadiness when walking, all of which may gradually get worse over time. Like people with juvenile Tay-Sachs, those with late-onset, or chronic, Tay-Sachs have one completely nonfunctional gene for hex A as well as one gene that produces some level of hex A. The greater the level of hex A produced, the less severe the disease.

Sometimes the effects of late-onset Tay-Sachs are chronic. This means that the symptoms continue at a moderate level for a long period of time as opposed to a rapid onset of symptoms that result in deterioration and an early death. However, because the physical decline is gradual, there is more time for mental effects to become obvious. Often people with late-onset and chronic Tay-Sachs live a normal life span, which is currently into the seventies.

MENTAL EFFECTS OF LATE-ONSET TAY-SACHS

Sixty percent of people with late-onset Tay-Sachs do not have serious mental symptoms. However, up to 40% of those with the late-onset form of the disease have **psychological** (related to the mind) difficulties related to changes that take place in the brain. Psychological problems can include **depression** (excessive sadness and gloom), **dementia** (mental confusion), **hallucinations** (seeing or hearing things that are not there), **paranoia** (unreasonable fear), and memory problems.

People with late-onset Tay-Sachs do not have as massive a buildup of lipid in their brain as do those who suffer from the other types of Tay-Sachs disease. In addition, often only certain parts of the brain are affected. Areas most likely to be affected include the **hippocampus** (a seahorse-shaped structure in the middle of the brain that processes memories), the **brain stem** (the area at the base of the brain that controls **reflexes** and involuntary functions such as breathing), and the **spinal cord** (the bundle of nerves running down the back that carry nerve signals to and from the brain). The area of the brain least likely to be affected is the **cerebral cortex**, the part of the brain responsible for high-level functions such as learning and reasoning.

GENETICS OF JUVENILE, CHRONIC, AND LATE-ONSET TAY-SACHS

Children with juvenile Tay-Sachs disease usually have one completely nonfunctional form of the gene for hex A on one copy of chromosome 15, but the defective gene on their other copy of chromosome 15 is not completely nonfunctional. Rather, it results in the production of a small amount of hex A but not enough to sustain normal functioning. Juvenile Tay-Sachs is caused by a particular type of genetic defect called the B1 variant. The B1 variant results in a form of the hex A enzyme that does have some activity, although it operates at a much lower level than normal. The most common cause of the B1 variant is a mutation called R178H, which is most commonly found in people of Portuguese ancestry. This mutation affects the area of the hex A protein that attaches to the GM2 ganglioside. Chronic Tay-Sachs is also frequently caused by the B1 variant.

There are two major mutations that are commonly linked to late-onset Tay-Sachs disease. The first mutation is called G269S and commonly occurs in the Ashkenazi Jewish population. The two parts of the hex A enzyme, the alpha subunit and the beta subunit, must join together to form a complete enzyme. In people with this mutation, the alpha subunit is unstable, so the two halves of hex A do not join together, and the enzyme is not functional.

The second mutation is called G250D. It is a change in a single base on the gene, which results in a nonfunctional enzyme. Both mutations lead to late-onset Tay-Sachs regardless of whether the person has one defective gene and one completely nonfunctioning gene, or if the person has two defective genes.

SANDHOFF DISEASE

There are a number of other lipid storage diseases that have symptoms and effects similar to those of Tay-Sachs disease. One such disorder, called Sandhoff disease, is closely related to Tay-Sachs disease. Sandhoff disease was identified in 1968 by a German chemist, Konrad Sandhoff. Children with Sandhoff disease have too little of both the hex A enzyme and another enzyme called hexosaminidase B (hex B), which also dissolves lipids.

Children with Sandhoff disease usually start to show symptoms when they are about six months old and show the same mental and physical symptoms as people with Tay-Sachs. However, in addition to the physical effects seen in regular Tay-Sachs disease, Sandhoff disease affects organs outside the nervous system, such as the liver, and leads to abnormal bone growth, in some cases producing an abnormally large head. Children with Sandhoff disease live about three years. Unlike Tay-Sachs disease, Sandhoff disease mostly occurs in non-Jewish populations and is not often seen in Jewish children.

DIAGNOSING
TAY-SACHS DISEASE

The symptoms of Tay-Sachs disease are well known. The muscle spasms and weakness, loss of motor skills, and other symptoms of Tay-Sachs are caused by damage to the nerve cells in the brain. However, these symptoms are not unique to Tay-Sachs disease. They occur in a wide variety of **neurological** (nerve and brain-related) diseases, as well as disorders caused by exposure to toxic chemicals. Doctors are faced with the challenge of figuring out if a person is suffering from Tay-Sachs disease instead of some other disorder. This chapter looks at how doctors go about diagnosing Tay-Sachs disease.

DIAGNOSING TAY-SACHS

One reason why diagnosing Tay-Sachs can be difficult is because the symptoms are typical of many other diseases, including multiple sclerosis, amyotrophic lateral sclerosis (ALS), and cystic fibrosis. In addition, the diagnosis is challenging because most of the victims of this disease are very young—babies and young children are usually unable to describe verbally how they are feeling.

Doctors rely on several techniques to identify a patient who is suffering from Tay-Sachs rather than another disease.

Among these tools are family history, visual observation, and testing. One of the important questions that doctors ask is whether a child with symptoms has parents who are Ashkenazi Jews. The doctor will also ask many questions about the child's family history to find out if any of the child's relatives has, or had, Tay-Sachs disease. If there are relatives who had children with the disease or who developed late-onset Tay-Sachs, this indicates that the gene for Tay-Sachs is present in the family lineage. This increases the chances that the child has Tay-Sachs.

One physical symptom that helps identify Tay-Sachs disease is the presence of the distinctive cherry-red spot on the retina. A doctor uses a device called an **ophthalmoscope**, an

FIGURE 4.1 A child is given an eye exam with an ophthalmoscope, which can be used to examine in the inside of the eye and the retina. A cherry-red spot on the retina is one symptom of Tay-Sachs disease.

instrument with a mirror that reflects light into the eye and a hole that enables the doctor to view the back of the eye to detect the spot. The retina contains many retinal nerve cells called ganglions. In children with Tay-Sachs disease, these nerve cells are deformed by the buildup of GM2 ganglioside. This affects the small pit in the back of the eye called the *fovea centralis*, the point at which vision is sharpest. Retinal ganglions are "pushed out of the way" at this point to maximize the sharpness of vision. When viewed through an ophthalmoscope, the spot looks red because of the healthy blood vessels present there, in contrast to the surrounding cells. This is not because it is defective, but because it is the only part of the retina that remains normal. This spot, however is not only found in Tay-Sachs disease but is also seen in babies suffering from several other rare diseases that affect nerve cells, such as Gaucher disease, Niemann-Pick disease, and Sandhoff disease.

Since patients suffering from juvenile and late-onset Tay-Sachs often have muscle wasting and weakness as their primary symptoms, doctors must be certain that the patient is not suffering from some other muscle-wasting disease. Therefore, doctors who suspect that a person has Tay-Sachs often order an enzyme assay and/or DNA test.

ENZYME ASSAYS

Assay is a word meaning "test." Enzyme assays measure the amount of enzyme present in a person's blood. In this type of test, a small amount of blood is drawn from a vein and analyzed in a laboratory to see how much of the hex A enzyme is present. There are different ways enzymes can be measured. One approach is to add a compound that causes the enzyme to react with the patient's blood. This compound is called the **substrate**. After a suitable period, the amount of substrate still present in the blood is measured. The more of the enzyme that is present in the blood, the less of the substrate that will remain. Thus, if there is a lot of substrate left, this proves that there is not much enzyme in the blood sample, and the patient may have Tay-Sachs disease. Another approach is to use an **immunoassay** test, a test that uses components of the immune system to identify the presence of a disease.

DNA SEQUENCING

The DNA test for Tay-Sachs obtains the sequence of the four bases: adenine, guanine, cytosine, and thymine. The sequence is examined to see if it is normal and is then compared to a variety of known mutations to see if it contains a recognizable mutation for Tay-Sachs disease. The patient's DNA is obtained from a blood or cell sample. The cell sample is acquired by removing some cells from the inside of the cheek by swabbing it with a tiny brush.

The Polymerase Chain Reaction

DNA testing starts with a process called the **polymerase chain reaction** (PCR). PCR can show the exact sequence of bases in a gene. These bases are the building blocks from which every gene is constructed. Combinations of the four bases in DNA—adenine (A), guanine (G), cytosine (C), and thymine (T)—appear in a different order in different genes. (For example, a sequence might be AAGCTT or AGTCA.) When geneticists look at this sequence, they can see whether any bases are missing from a gene or whether there are extra bases that do not belong there. PCR is based on an enzyme called DNA polymerase I. This enzyme is responsible for controlling the **synthesis** (manufacture) of DNA.

Each base on a strand of DNA attaches, or binds, to a complementary base, forming a base pair. For example, A binds with T, and C binds with G. Scientists can use this information to create identical strands of DNA from a tiny amount of DNA.

The amount of DNA obtained from a patient is very small. In order to sequence the DNA, scientists first make enough copies of it for testing. Reproducing the sample DNA involves the following steps:

1. **Denature the DNA**: When the base pairs are bound to each other, the DNA exists as a double strand that must be separated in order to duplicate both strands. The DNA is placed in the test tube and heated, causing the two strands of DNA to separate so that new, complementary bases can bind to each strand, creating two new strands of DNA. This process is called *denaturing*.

2. **Add primer**: Each single strand of DNA consists of a sequence of bases, and each base can bind to its complementary base. Next, a primer is added to the test tube. The primer is a short piece of DNA that attaches to the end of the strand of DNA and helps starts the process of assembling a second strand of DNA.

3. **Add bases and the polymerase enzyme**: Bases and the polymerase enzyme are also added to the test tube. The polymerase can "read" the bases on the strand of DNA. It moves down the strand of DNA, attaching the appropriate complementary base to each base on the strand of DNA. Another polymerase in the solution does the same thing to the other strand of DNA that was separated from the original double strand.

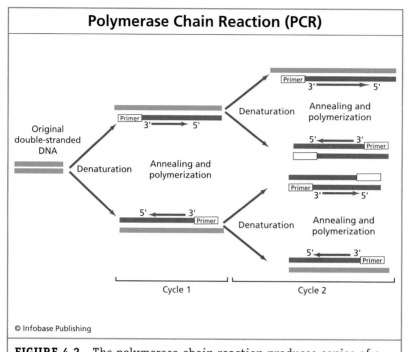

© Infobase Publishing

FIGURE 4.2   The polymerase chain reaction produces copies of a nucleotide sequence using primers for DNA synthesis.

When the polymerase is done, every single strand of DNA is now a double strand instead, because each single strand has had a complete set of complementary bases attached to it. Then the process of attaching a primer and using polymerase to attach complementary bases is repeated. This process can be repeated as many times as necessary until there are enough identical double strands of DNA in the test tube to allow for sequencing or other analysis.

Sequencing the DNA

Scientists can sequence the DNA using chemical or automated methods. When they sequence the DNA, they will be able to see exactly what bases make up each gene, so they will be able to tell if a gene does not have the correct sequences of bases and is, therefore, defective.

To sequence DNA, scientists go through the same steps they used for the PCR. This time, however, they add a tag or marker to the bases that allows them to be identified. For example, they may add a dye to each base that glows a particular color, such as red or green, when exposed to ultraviolet light. (Ultraviolet light is light at the extreme purple end of the color spectrum that is invisible to the naked eye, but causes certain colors to glow.) Marking the different bases this way makes it possible to identify them so that it is possible to see if they are all where they should be and in the right order.

The assembled DNA is then processed using a method that separates it according to size because this allows the scientists to tell where each base occurs in order. A method commonly used for this is called gel electrophoresis. In gel electrophoresis, a sample of the substance to be analyzed is injected into a gel and an electric current is run through it. This causes the molecules in the substance to move through the gel. The various sizes of the molecules cause them to move different distances through the gel. The shorter the sequence of bases is, the closer it is to the beginning of the strand. At the same time, the different colors in the sequenced segment tell scientists the order of the bases in each segment. In this way, scientists learn the order of bases in each segment that is sequenced and where each sequenced segment is located in order from the beginning of the strand. They then know the exact sequence of bases in the DNA that is being analyzed.

Automated machines called gene sequencers have been developed to perform this analysis and print out the results, making the process of gene sequencing much easier.

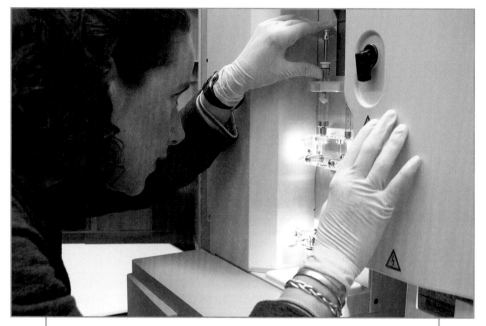

FIGURE 4.3 Researcher Elizabeth Gillanders, Ph.D., monitors a DNA sequencing machine. The machine enables scientists to print out the exact order of base pairs in an individual's DNA.

ENZYME ASSAY VERSUS DNA TESTING

Because DNA tests allow scientists to see the makeup of a person's unique DNA, it is a more accurate way of figuring out if a person has a defective gene. So, why don't geneticists simply use this test instead of an enzyme activity test? This sort of DNA testing has two drawbacks: (1) first, it can generate false positives—results that incorrectly appear to show a defect, and (2) it is only useful if testers are aware of the specific defect they should be looking for. In other words, screeners need to know that a certain pattern produced in the test represents a mutation that causes Tay-Sachs. For this reason, DNA testing is most useful in populations where common mutations are known, such as Ashkenazi Jews and French Canadians.

The fact that over 100 mutations have been discovered means it is likely that there are other mutations still to be discovered. The enzyme activity test is useful for discovering if a person has a problem producing hex A, but the person may turn out to have one of the less common genetic mutations. PCR is most useful when the ancestry of both parents is known.

NEWBORN TESTING

One reason that it is so challenging to find a cure or treatment for Tay-Sachs disease is that damage has already been done before the baby is even born. In fact, the destruction of brain cells caused by the lack of the hex A enzyme actually begins while the infant is still in the womb. The infants possess the defective gene at birth and their bodies are already suffering from the effects of not having the enzyme, although the buildup of GM2 ganglioside has not yet reached the point where symptoms appear.

Although treatments for Tay-Sachs are still in the experimental stages, someday it might be possible to improve the management of the disease. Many of the treatments that are being explored for Tay-Sachs disease are most effective when they are applied before the disease becomes advanced. There is little doubt that the earlier a disease is diagnosed, the better it can be managed. This is especially true of diseases such as Tay-Sachs that affect the brain. In the case of Tay-Sachs, though, it is not enough to fix the problem of GM2 ganglioside buildup: It must be tackled before the buildup damages brain cells.

In addition, some treatments such as bone marrow and stem cell implantation work better before the child's **immune system** has matured. Because the immune system destroys foreign particles that enter the body, it is often easier to introduce bone marrow or **stem cells** into the body when a baby is very young and its immune system is not fully developed. At that point, it is less likely that the marrow or the cells will be destroyed.

Currently, newborn testing is done using a small dab of blood that is usually obtained by pricking the baby's heel because its veins are too small to draw blood from them with a needle. Because of the importance of diagnosing metabolic diseases early, researchers are working to develop a number of tests that can be used to more accurately screen babies for a variety of lysosomal storage disorders, including Tay-Sachs disease. An example of a testing method that is being explored for use with newborns is *immunoassay* testing.

Immunoassay Testing

The term *immunoassay* means a test (assay) that uses components of the immune system (immuno). This type of testing relies on the basic way that elements in the immune system work. The immune system's function is to capture and destroy foreign particles and bacteria that get into a person's system. **Antibodies** are proteins that are part of the immune system. They are shaped like the letter Y; the open end of the Y attaches to foreign particles in the blood. Each antibody recognizes and attaches, or binds, to a specific type of foreign particle. Scientists use this behavior to develop tests.

In an immunoassay test, an identifying marker is attached to antibodies for the hex A enzyme. This could be a chemical that glows under ultraviolet light or a weak **radioactive**

FIGURE 4.4 This technician is using an Enzyme Linked ImmunoSorbent Assay (ELISA) test, which is an immunoassay test, to determine whether or not a patient has normal levels of the hex A enzyme.

element (an element that releases rays of energy) that can be detected with an instrument that measures radioactivity. This marked antibody is mixed with a sample of a person's blood. If there is hex A enzyme in the person's blood, the marked antibodies will attach themselves to it. The unattached antibodies are removed and scientific instruments are used to measure the amount of hex A enzyme/marked antibody that is left. If there is a normal amount of hex A enzyme, the person does not have Tay-Sachs. If there is a lower-than-normal amount of hex A, the person may be a carrier of the Tay-Sachs gene. If there is no hex A, the person may have Tay-Sachs disease, although DNA testing will most likely be done to confirm this diagnosis.

5

SCREENING FOR TAY-SACHS

Great advances have been made recently in DNA analysis technology and the identification of genetic mutations that cause diseases such as Tay-Sachs. One of the biggest benefits is that it has become possible to pinpoint individuals who have defective genes. This provides them with options, including conceiving a child who will not develop the disease. This chapter explains the various types of testing that can be done to identify both carriers and fetuses that test positive for Tay-Sachs disease.

THE IMPORTANCE OF KNOWING YOUR FAMILY'S MEDICAL HISTORY

A person's medical history can provide a wealth of information as to whether or not there are diseases that might affect them or their children in the future. There is more to understanding a family's medical history than just knowing whether their mother, father, brothers, and sisters have had any serious diseases. Knowing about any diseases or disorders a grandparent, aunt, uncle, cousin, niece, or nephew has had can also help patients and medical professionals to identify if there are any particular diseases to watch out for. Disorders such as heart disease and cancer result from a combination of genetic, environmental, and lifestyle factors.

Other diseases, such as Tay-Sachs, develop because of a genetic mutation on a single gene. In this case, a family history of the disease is a very important piece of information because it could alert a doctor to the possibility that a person would be likely to have a child with Tay-Sachs, leading to a quicker diagnosis.

It is important to know, however, that Tay-Sachs disease can still occur in a child whose family has no history of the disease. This is possible because mutations sometimes happen when chromosomes are duplicated during the creation of sperm and egg cells. An error that occurs randomly as opposed to being inherited is called a **spontaneous mutation**. It is also true that just because a disease has affected a family member, it does not mean that every child in the family will inherit or develop it. Knowing that there is a family history of a disease equips people to take precautions that can benefit them and their children. The best way to collect information for a family medical history is to talk to relatives about diseases they and other relatives have had. It is important to write this information down and keep it for future reference.

HOW GREAT IS THE RISK?

Family history plays an important role in many disorders. With Tay-Sachs disease, an ethnic background can play a role in how likely someone is to carry the gene for the disease. The likelihood that one is a carrier for Tay-Sachs increases if a close family member has been affected by the disease, as shown in the following list:

◆ There is about a 65% chance that a person is a carrier of a gene for Tay-Sachs if a brother or sister has the disease.

◆ There is a 50% chance if a person has a niece or nephew who has the disease.

◆ There is a 33% chance if a person's aunt or uncle had the disease.

◆ There is a 25% chance if a person has a first cousin with Tay-Sachs disease.

If someone finds out that they are likely to be a carrier of Tay-Sachs disease, they may worry about passing it on to their children. For this reason, many people who are at risk have themselves and their partner screened for the Tay-Sachs gene prior to having children. They may wish to have testing done when they are pregnant to make sure that the baby will not have Tay-Sachs disease. Tay-Sachs testing is not a routine part of a standard medical exam, so members of a high-risk population or those who have a family history of the disease may want to discuss the Tay-Sachs test with their doctor or a genetic counselor.

It is important to understand that if both partners have a defective gene for hex A, every child they produce will have the same chance of developing Tay-Sachs. There is a 25% chance that a child born to two parents who both have the gene for Tay-Sachs will have Tay-Sachs disease. This is true because the condition of the first child has no effect on what genes the second child will receive. Every time a child is conceived, that child will have a 25% chance of getting two defective genes, a 25% chance of getting two healthy genes, and a 50% chance of getting one healthy gene and one defective gene—thus, he or she will be a carrier.

WHAT IS GENETIC COUNSELING?

Genetic counseling is a process in which family members meet with a professional counselor and get information and support in dealing with genetic diseases. Genetic counselors are trained in both the field of genetics and the field of counseling. Many of these counselors have a background in nursing, biology, public health, psychology, or social work. Genetic counselors are certified by the National Society for Genetic Counselors. It is important to make sure that the genetic counselor is certified by the American Board of Genetic Counselors because certification verifies that they have had appropriate training in both genetics and counseling.

Genetic counselors work in a variety of places, including hospitals and medical centers, genetic screening centers, and private doctors' offices. Counselors provide information about genetic disorders and the likelihood of a person inheriting one; options for testing; information about how the tests are performed; and options for dealing with the situation if the couple conceives a child who has Tay-Sachs. The purpose of genetic counseling is to provide a couple with the information they need to make personal and medical decisions.

What Happens in Genetic Counseling?

A genetic counselor will ask a patient for information about his or her medical history—including that of both immediate family members and more distant relations. The counselor may also do a physical exam and will most likely recommend specific tests. If the results of the Tay-Sachs tests are positive, the counselor will then explain what the results mean, how the defective gene was inherited, and what

FIGURE 5.1 This pregnant couple is seeking genetic counseling. People often seek genetic counseling in order to get information and support regarding genetic diseases that they may pass on to their children.

the defect could mean in terms of having children. If both partners are testing because they are planning to have a child, and they both turn out to be carriers of the defective gene, the counselor will explain the options for having children. It is important to understand that counselors will provide the information a patient needs to make decisions, but they will not tell the patient which decision to make.

Finding a Genetic Counselor

There are several ways a person can go about finding a genetic counselor. First, they can check with their primary care doctor, who may be able to recommend a counselor. There are also a number of organizations that can provide lists of genetic counselors and screening centers. These include organizations specializing in Tay-Sachs support such as the National Tay-Sachs and Allied Diseases Association; organizations that run genetic screening programs for Tay-Sachs such as the Mount Sinai Center for Jewish Genetics; Jewish community groups; and the National Society of Genetic Counselors.

Health insurance providers can also provide a list of genetic counselors that are covered by insurance plans. Some people are reluctant to have genetic testing done through their insurance company because they are afraid that if a genetic problem is found, the company will drop them from coverage or charge them higher premiums. If they have an employer-paid insurance plan, there is also some danger that the information will get back to the employer. Although there are laws that are supposed to guarantee confidentiality (secrecy) of the patient's medical information, there have been instances where information has been shared with employers as part of the billing process. In some cases, this can lead to employers who do not understand the nature of a disease discriminating (acting unfairly) against employees who test positively for that disease. To help combat this problem, the U.S. Congress passed the Genetic Information Nondiscrimination Act, and President George W. Bush signed it into law in May 2008. The law protects people against discrimination from employers or insurance companies because they have tested positive for a disease-causing gene on a genetic test.

PRENATAL TESTING

If a couple becomes pregnant and they are both members of a population at risk for Tay-Sachs, they may want to test the fetus to make sure it does not have the disease. This is another area where working with a genetic counselor can be helpful.

Prenatal means "before birth." Prenatal testing is carried out while the baby is still a **fetus** developing in the mother's womb. The test is done when both parents are known to be carriers of the gene for Tay-Sachs. When couples who are carriers of the gene conceive a child, there is a 1 in 4 chance that the child will develop the disease. Prenatal testing allows parents to find out if the fetus has two copies of the gene for Tay-Sachs. If so, the infant will, inevitably, develop the disease.

There are two approaches to prenatal testing. The first approach is called **chorionic villus sampling** (CVS). This type of testing takes place between the tenth and twelfth weeks of pregnancy. A small amount of tissue is removed from projections called *chorionic villi* that stick out from the **placenta** (the organ in the womb that attaches the fetus to the mother's blood supply so that it can receive nourishment and eliminate waste). This tissue is tested using DNA analysis.

The other approach is called is *amniocentesis.* This test is used between the fifteenth and eighteenth weeks of pregnancy. In this type of testing, a needle is used to remove some of the fluid in which the fetus floats in the womb. Cells in the fluid are then screened using DNA analysis.

However, determining that the fetus has Tay-Sachs disease is not the end of the issue. The question then becomes, what options do the parents have? Since there is no cure for infantile Tay-Sachs and the child will face great suffering and ultimately die, one option is to terminate the pregnancy through an **abortion** (the removal of the fetus from the womb to end the pregnancy). However, abortion, even for

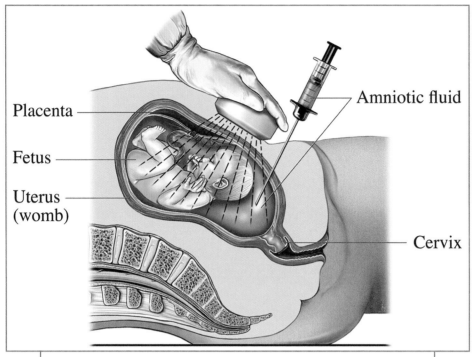

Placenta

Fetus

Uterus
(womb)

Amniotic fluid

Cervix

FIGURE 5.2 In amniocentesis, a physician uses a needle to draw a sample of amniotic fluid from the uterus. The physician uses ultrasound in order to avoid contact with the fetus.

the most humane of reasons, raises ethical issues for many people.

PRECONCEPTION SCREENING

One of the most common reasons that couples who want to have children seek genetic counseling is because they come from a population that is at high risk for passing on Tay-Sachs or a similar disease. In this case, the couple will most likely have themselves tested to see if they are carriers. If they are both positive for Tay-Sachs disease, the counselor can assist them with their decision. Couples who are both carriers have several options other than not having children.

In Vitro Fertilization

In vitro fertilization (IVF) techniques can be used to ensure that a baby conceived by a couple does not have Tay-Sachs. IVF is a process commonly used in fertility clinics to help couples who are having trouble conceiving a baby. *In vitro* means "in glass" in Latin. It refers to the processes carried out in laboratories because such procedures are often performed in test tubes or shallow glass dishes called petri dishes.

When performing in vitro fertilization, eggs are removed from a woman's ovaries with a syringe. They are fertilized in the laboratory with the father's sperm. Eventually, **embryos** form. (An embryo is a cluster of cells that will develop into a fetus and result in a baby.)

With carriers of the Tay-Sachs gene, the next step may be **pre-implantation testing**, in which the embryos are tested for the presence of a defective HEXA gene. The embryos whose test results are normal are then implanted into the woman's uterus (womb).

The embryos are implanted, or placed, into the woman's womb, where one or more of them may develop into a fetus. From that point on, the pregnancy proceeds like any other normal pregnancy.

Pre-implantation testing has been used successfully with carriers of Tay-Sachs as well as a number of other fatal diseases such as *cystic fibrosis* (a genetic disease in which thick mucus builds up in the lungs) and *sickle cell anemia* (a disease common in African Americans where red blood cells are misshapen).

This has proved to be a highly successful way of avoiding having a child with Tay-Sachs. It allows two people who are carriers to have children without fear of passing on the disease. It avoids both the pain of having a child who suffers and dies of Tay-Sachs disease and having to make the decision about whether or not to have an abortion. However, the procedure is very expensive and, therefore, only available to couples who can afford it.

Another approach to reducing the chances of having a child with Tay-Sachs when both parents are carriers is to perform IVF with eggs or sperm donated by someone who does not carry the genes for Tay-Sachs disease. Assuming that the donor has been screened to verify that he or she does not have the disease, the baby will have only one parent with a defective HEXA gene. Because two defective genes must be inherited for a child to have Tay-Sachs, in most cases this guarantees the child will not have the disease. There are two disadvantages to this approach: (1) the resulting baby is biologically related to only one of its parents, which may cause issues in the family, and (2) IVF is

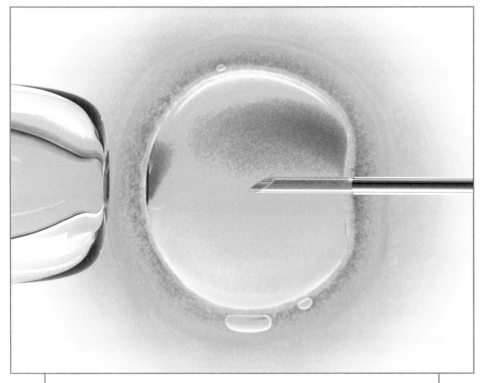

FIGURE 5.3   In the process of in vitro fertilization, eggs and sperm are joined outside the womb in a laboratory setting. If an egg is successfully fertilized, it may then be moved to the uterus.

very expensive, so it is a practical approach only for couples who are financially well off.

CARRIER SCREENING

Because of the significant likelihood that the child of two carriers of the defective gene will develop Tay-Sachs disease, carrier testing plays an important role in reducing the number of children born with Tay-Sachs. Indeed, prior to 1970, Tay-Sachs occurred in 1 out of every 4,000 children born to Ashkenazi Jewish parents. However, from the 1970s through the present day, more than 1 million Ashkenazi Jews, mostly in the United States and Israel, have undergone carrier testing. This has led to a significant drop in the number of children with Tay-Sachs disease born to Ashkenazi Jews in those countries.

How Does Carrier Screening Work?

Carrier screening is carried out by geneticists. The first mass screening programs for Tay-Sachs were performed in the 1970s and 1980s. At that time, screeners relied on a blood test that measured the activity of hex A in white blood cells or serum (the clear fluid in which blood cells float). If there was little hex A activity, the screeners knew that a person had a defective gene for hex A. In the 1990s and 2000s, many types of genetic defects were identified for the HEXA gene. While some of these mutations appear primarily in one ethnic group, such as Ashkenazi Jews or French Canadians, people of every ethnic group and race carry a genetic mutation for hex A.

Now that the mutations are known, geneticists can use advanced gene sequencing technology to identify these defects directly. In gene sequencing, chemicals and biological compounds are combined with a person's DNA to reveal the components that make up a particular gene. Techniques such as polymerase chain reaction (PCR) are used to screen potential carrier's DNA. In this way, it is possible for geneticists to find out whether or not a person's HEXA gene is normal or has a particular mutation that will keep the gene from functioning properly.

To ensure accuracy, many geneticists perform both enzyme activity and gene sequencing tests. If a person has a mutation not on the list of diseases being screened for, a poor result in the enzyme assay will alert screeners to that fact. This is especially important when testing people in populations other than Ashkenazi Jews because there is a higher likelihood that an unidentified mutation might exist. However, performing just the enzyme assay is not enough. If a poor result in the enzyme assay is the result of some factor other than a defective HEXA gene, the researchers will pick up on it when they see that the person's HEXA gene is normal in the DNA test. Thus, double-checking by using both tests is important and necessary.

Screening for Marriage Partners

Some Orthodox Jews (the most conservative sect of Judaism) rely on screening to make sure that two people with the gene for Tay-Sachs disease do not become romantically involved and subsequently get married.

There is an organization called Dor Yeshorim, based in Brooklyn, New York, with offices in Israel, that offers screening services for this purpose. (*Dor Yeshorim* means "straight or reliable generation.") The organization was founded in the 1980s by Rabbi Joseph Ekstein, who had lost four of his five children to Tay-Sachs disease. The organization tests for a number of other fatal diseases that are also carried as recessive traits on genes. A simple blood test is all that is necessary to test for Tay-Sachs and nine other fatal recessive genetic diseases. The testing is done anonymously, meaning that the identity of those tested is kept secret. Those tested are then given a PIN (personal identification number), like that used at ATM machines or online to access an account. When a couple is thinking about having children, they can use their PIN to see whether or not they have the gene for Tay-Sachs. If both of them have the gene, then they know that there is a risk the child will develop the disease.

Pros and Cons of Mass Screening

Those in favor of mass screening point to the fact that the number of cases of Tay-Sachs disease has dropped radically in populations such as Ashkenazi Jews who have implemented mass screening programs. However, mass screening programs have raised a number of issues. One problem with them is the fear that efforts to keep the results confidential may not work: Those who test positive for genetic diseases may fear that their information may be obtained by their health insurance company anyway with the result that—despite the 2008 law prohibiting insurance companies from discriminating against those who test positive for genetic diseases—the insurer may deny coverage or charge more for their policy.

Those who oppose mass screening claim that it is a form of **eugenics**—the selective mating of individuals to develop specific genetic qualities. Those who favor such screening point out, however, that they are not selecting individuals on the basis of specific traits, but are merely identifying an otherwise unidentifiable trait that could lead to a specific fatal disease. This has no effect on choosing people with any traits to achieve any particular goal.

The issue of eugenics is a societal issue—one that affects the whole community. Other impacts of genetic screening may be more personal. If a person finds out that he or she is a carrier of the Tay-Sachs gene, it may affect how that person deals with relationships. For example, a person might be reluctant either to get involved with another person or get married for fear of passing on the disease to their children. Some people may be afraid of how the other person will react when they admit they are a carrier. Sometimes the test results cause anger and depression in people. For this reason, it is important to work with a genetic counselor when having genetic testing done.

But sometimes getting test results can turn out to be less stressful than not knowing, because awareness of the problem can help a person take control of the situation. Furthermore, if the result is negative, then a person will know that they no longer have to worry about this issue. It is important to remember that people of all types and different backgrounds have defects, and a variety of diseases run in families. As science continues to advance, increasing numbers of options will become available that allow people to have children in ways that minimize the chances of passing on Tay-Sachs or other fatal genetic disorders.

DIRECT-TO-CONSUMER TESTING

One area of genetic testing that is generating a lot of interest is direct-to-consumer testing. In this case, manufacturers or laboratories provide test kits or testing services directly to the consumer who performs the test at home or provides a sample to a lab. Direct-to-consumer genetic testing is still new and there are a limited number of tests available on the market. Most of these direct-to-consumer tests are available over the Internet. Direct-to-consumer testing raises a number of issues such as how to guarantee that the kit or laboratory is reliable and accurate. The advantage of home testing is that there are no worries about confidentiality. No one else will know the results. One major disadvantage, though, especially in the case of extremely serious diseases like Tay-Sachs, is the lack of support from a genetic counselor who can help a person deal with the results if the test turns out positive for a defective gene.

6

RESEARCHING
TREATMENTS

Although there is currently no effective treatment for Tay-Sachs disease, researchers are currently exploring ways to avoid, treat, and possibly cure the disease. Many experiments have led to an understanding of the biochemical factors that cause Tay-Sachs disease. This chapter discusses the most significant of them.

UNLOCKING THE SECRETS OF TAY-SACHS

Biochemistry is the study of how chemical compounds are produced and how they behave in living organisms. Before treatments can be developed for a disease like Tay-Sachs, the biochemical process that produces the disease must be understood. This information can then be used to develop approaches to address the causes of the disease. In order to realize how far the research has come, it is important to learn the history of this research.

In 1968, John A. Balint and Emilios C. Kyriakides of the Albany Medical College in Albany, New York, studied the red blood cells of 9 patients with Tay-Sachs disease and 14 control subjects. (Control subjects are healthy people who provide a group against which researchers can compare the affected individuals.) This allows researchers to pinpoint the differences that occur in the sick people as compared to the healthy control group members during the research period. They analyzed the blood cells of both groups and found that the cells of the children with Tay-Sachs contained approximately 25% more protein, hexosamine, the **amino acids** threonine and serine (amino acids are the molecules that build up proteins), and **sialic acid** (a building block of glycoproteins like GM2 ganglioside) than the cells of the control subjects. The researchers recognized that the increase in these elements meant that the red blood cells had an excess amount of a glycoprotein or proteins. This led them to conclude that the build-up of lipid in Tay-Sachs disease was related to an excess of a glycoprotein, which was later identified as GM2 ganglioside.

In 1969, Shintaro Okada and John S. O'Brien of the University of California at San Diego School of Medicine noticed that the alpha subunit of the hexosaminidase enzyme was missing in people with Tay-Sachs. They used **starch-gel electrophoresis** to separate the various components of hexosaminidase. In gel electrophoresis, a sample of the substance to be analyzed is injected into a gel. An electric current is run through the gel that causes the molecules in the substance to move. The different sizes of the molecules determine how far they are able to move through the gel. Therefore, the different molecules become separated from each other and can be identified by the pattern they make in the gel. In this way, Okada and O'Brien's study showed that the alpha subunit of hexosaminidase was missing in the brain, liver, kidney, skin, blood plasma (the liquid part of blood), and white blood cells of patients with Tay-Sachs disease.

In 1983, I.E. Conzelmann, R. Navon, and K. Sandhoff of the Institute of Chemistry and Biochemistry at the University of Bonn, Germany, and H.J. Kytzia of the Sackler School of Medicine at Tel-Aviv University, Israel, developed a highly sensitive test for how well patients with low levels of hexosa-minidase could break down GM2 ganglioside. Through this test, they were able to show a relationship between the levels of hex A enzyme and the severity of Tay-Sachs disease. Their work clarified the difference in the level of hexosamini-dase A present in patients with infantile Tay-Sachs disease and those with late-onset Tay-Sachs.

In 1988, R. Myerowitz and F.C. Costigan of the National Institute of Health and Digestive and Kidney Diseases in Bethesda, Maryland, identified the genetic mutation that most commonly causes Tay-Sachs disease in Ashkenazi Jews—a segment of four base pairs inserted in the HEXA gene. This mutation tells the body to stop constructing the alpha subunit of the hex A enzyme before it should.

The rate at which new HEXA mutations were discovered was increased by two factors. First, in the 1980s, new techniques were developed for sequencing DNA, such as the polymerase chain reaction and gel electrophoresis. Second, the **Human Genome Project**, started in 1990 with the goal of sequencing the entire DNA that is contained in a single human body, generated a great wave of interest in genetics. The need for a faster way to sequence DNA resulted in the development of the first automated gene sequencers. The automated machines sped up the process of sequencing genes and allowed researchers to find mutations at a much greater rate than when sequencing DNA by manual methods. By 2007, over 100 distinct mutations of the HEXA gene had been discovered by researchers worldwide.

MAKING A TAY-SACHS MOUSE

Before scientists can develop effective treatments for a disease, they first must have a thorough understanding of how the disease develops in the body. They need to know a lot more than what the symptoms are and what progressive course the disease takes. They need to know what chemical and biological elements in the body interact with each other, and how the interactions take place, in order to figure out ways to alter the processes that produce the disease.

One of the ways that scientists approach such a problem is to study the disease in animals. In the 1990s, scientists in the United States, France, and Canada all independently developed mice that were useful for studying Tay-Sachs disease. Their research projects have led to a much better understanding of how Tay-Sachs affects the brain and body. For instance, it has allowed researchers to observe the changes that take place in the brain as the disease progresses.

M.F. Seldin and his colleagues, working at the Duke University Medical Center in 1991, established that the mouse equivalent of the HEXA gene is located on mouse chromosome 9. This paved the way for developing an animal model of Tay-Sachs disease. In 1994, M. Taniike and colleagues at the University of North Carolina, Chapel Hill, succeeded in disrupting the gene responsible for producing hex A in mice. This produced the same symptoms seen in people with Tay-Sachs disease.

Animal models are useful for more than just gaining an understanding of a disease. The production of "Tay-Sachs" mice provided a way to test possible approaches to treating Tay-Sachs disease in a living organism. Researchers have been able to try out different therapeutic approaches, such as those that will be discussed in this chapter.

BONE MARROW AND STEM CELL IMPLANTATION

What if we could replace defective gene cells with cells that contain a correctly functioning gene? One scientific approach is to repair damaged cells by inserting a correctly functioning gene into them. There is, however, another approach—to insert cells with a correctly functioning gene into a patient's body. To treat Tay-Sachs disease, **bone marrow transplantation** and **embryonic stem cell replacement therapy** both rely on replacing cells in the patient's brain that contain a nonfunctioning gene with cells that contain a correctly functioning gene.

In the case of Tay-Sachs disease, if these cells take root in the brain and grow and reproduce like the patient's own cells, they will produce the missing hex A enzyme needed to break down GM2 ganglioside. This can be accomplished with the use of **stem cells**. Stem cells are immature cells produced in the bone marrow of the arm and leg bones. These cells have not yet fully developed the characteristics of particular types of cells such as a red blood cells, liver cells, muscle cells, and so on. When the body needs new cells, these immature cells travel to the tissue where they are needed. Once they arrive, they change into the specific type of cell, such as a liver or blood cell. Once a stem cell has changed into a particular type of mature cell, it cannot change again and permanently remains the type of cell it has matured into. This is the standard method the body uses to replace cells as needed.

Scientists have developed experimental treatments for a variety of diseases, including lipid storage disorders such as Tay-Sachs, that rely on this ability of stem cells to change into specific types of cells. Experiments in mice have demonstrated that newly introduced stem cells will spread throughout the brain. This is crucial to developing a successful treatment for diseases such as Tay-Sachs. In these types of diseases, the cells that need to be replaced are widespread and not located in one specific area of the brain. Stem cells can be used as-is from healthy donors or they can be genetically engineered in laboratories to produce specific chemicals such as the hex A enzyme. Experiments on mice have demonstrated that stem cells will secrete the hex A enzyme and the enzyme produced does, indeed, break down GM2 ganglioside.

There are two basic types of stem cell treatments: *bone marrow transplants*, in which stem cells from one person, called a donor, are transplanted, or placed, into the body of a patient; and *embryonic stem cell replacement therapy*, in which the stem cells are obtained from an embryo or the umbilical cord blood of a newborn baby.

Bone Marrow Transplantation

Bone marrow contains stem cells that travel through the bloodstream to tissue where new cells are needed. Because of this ability, stem cells have been used in experimental treatments since the 1980s. The most well-established use of bone marrow transplantation is to treat certain types of cancer, such as leukemia (a type of immune system cancer in which white blood cells multiply out of control). However, bone marrow transplants are being tested for use in other types of diseases.

The basic process in bone marrow transplantation is as follows. The patient's own bone marrow is destroyed using radiation treatment (exposing it to beams of energy) or **chemotherapy** (strong chemicals that kill fast-growing cells like those in bone marrow). Then a sample of bone marrow that contains healthy cells is removed from the donor's bone and implanted into the patient's bone. Hopefully, the new bone marrow starts producing healthy stem cells that will travel throughout the body, where they mature into adult cells.

In Tay-Sachs disease, the goal is for the stem cells to travel to the patient's brain. The resulting cells would have the genetic structure of the donor's cells, not the patient's

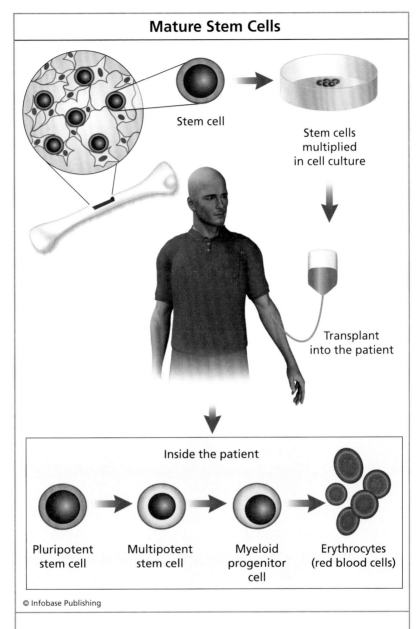

Mature Stem Cells

Stem cell

Stem cells multiplied in cell culture

Transplant into the patient

Inside the patient

| Pluripotent stem cell | Multipotent stem cell | Myeloid progenitor cell | Erythrocytes (red blood cells) |

© Infobase Publishing

FIGURE 6.1   Stem cells from bone marrow may be used to treat patients with cancer. Similar treatments are being tested for genetic diseases such as Tay-Sachs.

cells. Therefore, they would have a fully functioning gene for hex A instead of a defective one. The production of the hex A enzyme would help the patient avoid the ravaging effects of Tay-Sachs disease.

Researchers are investigating the feasibility of using bone marrow transplants in animal models, such as Tay-Sachs mice. This would allow doctors to address both the short-term and long-term needs of the patient.

Embryonic Stem Cell Replacement Therapy

Many researchers believe that embryonic stem cells show more promise for treating diseases than adult stem cells obtained from bone marrow. Embryonic stem cells are obtained from embryos (fertilized egg cells) in a very early phase of development. One reason for this is that embryonic stem cells are able to change into many more types of cells than the adult stem cells that are used in bone marrow transplantation. Embryonic stem cells can be obtained from four sources:

◆ **Leftover embryos from in vitro fertility clinics:** Fertility clinics produce more embryos than are actually implanted during fertility treatments because the treatment is not always successful the first time. The excess embryos that are not used are usually destroyed.

◆ **Embryos from terminated pregnancies:** As with leftover embryos from fertility treatments, aborted embryos are disposed. Instead, they could be used as a source of embryonic stem cells.

◆ **Early stage embryos created in laboratories:** In this process, sperm and egg cells are combined in the laboratory and allowed to develop until they form a ball of cells called a **blastocyst**, a process that takes about four or five days. Stem cells can be removed from the blastocyst, which is then destroyed before it reaches the stage at which it would be recognized as an embryo.

◆ **The umbilical cord blood of newborn babies:** Stem cells circulate through a baby's blood as it develops in the womb. The umbilical cord is a tube that links the fetus to the mother's blood supply so that it can get nutrients from its mother's bloodstream during pregnancy. Stem cells are carried along with this blood. When a baby is born, the blood in the umbilical cord contains stem cells.

Using stem cells from the first three sources has proved to be controversial (see the sidebar). However, the use of stem cells from umbilical cord blood is considered acceptable by most people because it does not involve the destruction of embryos.

In this approach, normal, healthy stem cells from umbilical cord blood are introduced into the patient's body, usually using an **intravenous**, or IV, device. In this approach, a solution containing the cells drips through a needle into the patient's vein. The cells travel through the bloodstream to the patient's brain, where, hopefully, they will develop into healthy hex A–producing cells. A number of patients with Tay-Sachs disease have been given experimental stem cell implantation treatment. Some improvement in neurological symptoms has been noted. This approach seems to show promise for halting continued degeneration, but the research is still in very early stages.

In one project, a team of researchers at Duke University, Durham, North Carolina, led by Dr. Joanne Kurtzberg,

(continues on page 84)

THE EMBRYONIC STEM CELL CONTROVERSY

The use of embryonic stems cells to treat diseases has caused a great deal of controversy. Many people and groups object to destroying embryos to treat patients. Some Christian groups—though not all of them—object to using embryos on the grounds that an embryo becomes a person at the moment of conception. Other religious groups, such as the Jewish and Islamic religions, do not object to using cells derived from embryos as long as they are less than 40 days old.

Those in favor of using embryonic stem cells believe that throwing away embryos from abortions and fertility treatments instead of using them to save lives is wasteful and unnecessarily condemns the victims of disease to suffering. Since the embryos have already been created and are going to be disposed of anyway, using them to treat disease would be more beneficial, and possibly more respectful.

In 2001, President George W. Bush signed a bill that restricted the federal government from funding new lines of stem cells. A stem cell line is made up of stem cells that are all descendants of a particular batch. This restriction on federal funding means that many research groups in the United States cannot get funding because they need to use new lines of stems cells. Those in favor of using embryonic stem cells to treat disease believe that these restrictions have caused the United States to fall behind in the development of new treatments for diseases such as Tay-Sachs disease, Alzheimer's disease, Type 1 diabetes, **Parkinson's disease**, cystic fibrosis, and multiple sclerosis. This has led to a number of U.S. scientists going to other countries to work. Proponents of embryonic stem cell treatments fear that the development of

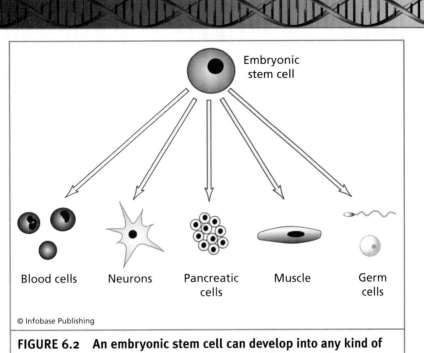

© Infobase Publishing

FIGURE 6.2 **An embryonic stem cell can develop into any kind of cell, such as blood cells, neurons, pancreatic cells, muscle cells, and germ cells.**

successful treatments in other countries that are unavailable in the United States may ultimately lead to rich Americans going to other countries to obtain treatment for diseases, while poor and middle-class Americans will not have access to cures for such diseases.

The use of embryonic stem cells from umbilical cord blood avoids much of this controversy. However, if successful stem cell treatments are developed for many diseases, there is a real possibility that there will not be a sufficient amount of stem cells available from this source. Therefore, the controversy continues.

(continued from page 81)

performed successful experiments using stem cells from umbilical cord blood. The Duke research has shown that the treatment is more likely to be successful and have fewer side effects in newborns than in older children. Thus, this method may best be used in combination with newborn screening. The Duke research has also demonstrated that umbilical cord stem cells seem to work better than stem cells from bone marrow. They travel to the brain faster, and it has been proved that they can change into brain cells. In addition, stem cells have produced improvement in Tay-Sachs disease patients two to four months sooner than bone marrow transplants. They are also less likely to cause a negative reaction from the patient's immune system, because they are much less mature than bone marrow stem cells.

Adult stem cells must be closely matched to the patient's blood type or they will be attacked by the patient's immune system. In contrast, embryonic stem cells only have to have a few elements in common with the patient. This makes it easier to find a donor for a sick child and can sometimes be done in as little as a week's time. This means that potentially more children could be treated sooner, minimizing the effects of the disease. Since both age and severity of the symptoms at the time of treatment affect the outcome, shortening the time before treatment is a crucial issue.

ENZYME REPLACEMENT THERAPY

One solution for people who do not have hex A enzyme would be simply to inject them with it. Of course, the enzyme would have to be injected at regular intervals. However, people today take regular injections for other diseases such as Type 1 (insulin-dependent) diabetes. For exactly this reason, enzyme replacement therapy is being researched for a whole range of lipid storage disorders, but there is still a long way to go before such treatments are likely to be approved by the U.S. Food and Drug Administration (FDA) for general usage.

Most of the hex A enzyme manufactured for therapeutic purposes is produced in vitro by using genetically engineered cells from the ovaries of Chinese hamsters. These cells are inserted with human DNA for producing the hex A protein. Scientists do this by using **recombinant** DNA technology. (*Recombinant* simply means "recombined.") Scientists make recombinant DNA by inserting a fragment of DNA at a specific point on a strand of DNA in a cell. The cell will then make the necessary protein encoded in that piece of DNA.

To insert the new DNA, scientists use **plasmids**. Plasmids are small rings of DNA found in bacteria. Bacteria use plasmids to transfer their DNA to other bacteria. Scientists can use plasmids to transfer good genes into patients who have genes that are defective. This process involves the following nine steps:

1. A technique such as polymerase chain reaction (PCR) is used to create the strands of DNA to be transferred.
2. The enzyme is used to cut a piece out of the ring of plasmid DNA.
3. The cutout DNA is replaced with the new DNA.
4. The plasmids are placed into containers with the cells to be "infected."
5. The plasmids then transfer the new DNA to the cells, and the cells start to produce the new protein, in this case hex A.
6. The cells are *cloned* so that there are an adequate number of them.
7. The infected cells produce hex A.

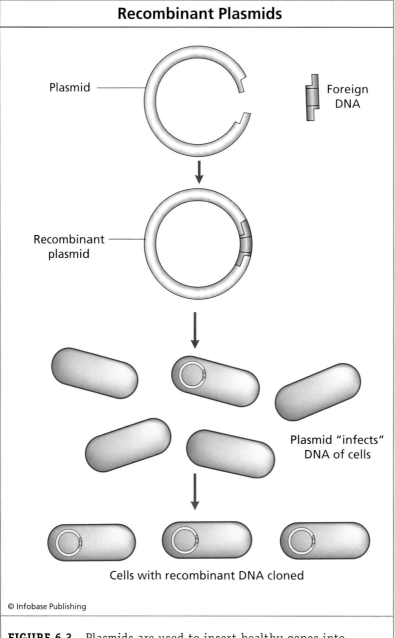

Recombinant Plasmids

Plasmid

Foreign DNA

Recombinant plasmid

Plasmid "infects" DNA of cells

Cells with recombinant DNA cloned

© Infobase Publishing

FIGURE 6.3   Plasmids are used to insert healthy genes into patients whose genes are defective.

8. The hex A produced by the cells in the laboratory is purified so that it is suitable for infusing intravenously (injected slowly into a vein) into patients.
9. The hex A is given to the patient intravenously.

There is a problem with this approach in the treatment of Tay-Sachs disease, however. The disease primarily affects the brain, and the brain is protected by the **blood-brain barrier**. The blood-brain barrier is a layer of tightly packed cells that line the blood vessels of the brain and act as a filtering system. Their job is to keep foreign particles and *toxic* (harmful) substances circulating in the blood from reaching the brain. This is helpful for filtering out dangerous *bacteria* (single-celled organisms) that could cause infection or a toxic chemical a person has come in contact with. However, sometimes the blood-brain barrier also filters out useful substances. This is the case with the hex A enzyme.

The hex A enzyme is composed of atoms, which are basic chemical elements such as carbon, hydrogen, oxygen, and nitrogen. Atoms combine to form larger units called molecules. Different combinations and arrangements of atoms give molecules particular properties. Some molecules are small—composed of only a small number of atoms. However, the hex A molecule is large, with many groups of atoms attached to it. In fact, it is too large to pass through the blood-brain barrier to reach the brain. Researchers have tried to get around this problem by using **cerebrospinal fluid** to deliver the enzyme. (This fluid circulates around the brain and through the spinal chord. Among other things, it helps protect nerve cells by acting as a shock absorber.) Because this fluid continually washes over the brain cells, researchers have tried putting the hex A enzyme directly into it. Still, the molecule turned out to be too large to deliver

THERAPEUTIC VERSUS REPRODUCTIVE CLONING

Most people think of cloning as the copying of the cells of animals or people from one of their parent's cells. This type of cloning is called *reproductive cloning*. In reproductive cloning, genetic material from the cells of a donor is inserted into the fertilized egg from which the native DNA has been removed. The egg then divides and eventually produces an embryo. The first successful cloning of a mammal was accomplished by Ian Wilmot of the Roslin Institute in Scotland in 1996. He cloned a sheep named "Dolly" from a cell taken from an adult sheep. Dolly was healthy and gave birth to a total of six lambs in 1998, 1999, and 2000. In 2001, when she was five years old, she began to suffer from diseases commonly seen in old animals, such as arthritis. In 2003, Dolly developed lung cancer and had to be *euthanized* (humanely killed). Although Dolly suffered from *premature* (early) aging because she had been created from a cell of an adult sheep, the successful cloning of a mammal caused a great deal of concern about the potential to clone human beings.

Therapeutic cloning is different from reproductive cloning. In therapeutic cloning, cells with native or genetically engineered DNA are stimulated to divide and reproduce in the lab. This merely produces more cells, all of which have DNA that is identical to the original cells. The cells do not grow into a complete animal. This process of "cloning" cells allows scientists to (1) make an adequate supply of cells with known and predictable characteristics for use in medical procedures, and (2) genetically engineer cells to produce a substance, such as the hex A enzyme, and then make more copies of those cells in order to have enough to produce an adequate amount of the substance for therapeutic use. Therapeutic cloning of cells is an important tool in developing adequate supplies of therapeutic compounds.

this way. Although the hex A actually got into the brain, the molecule was still too large to pass through the nerve cells' membrane into the cells.

SUBSTRATE DEPRIVATION THERAPY

The previously discussed therapies address the problem of Tay-Sachs by trying to replace the hex A enzyme either directly or through changing the patient's DNA so that the person produces the hex A enzyme. **Substrate deprivation therapy** takes a different approach. It is aimed at slowing down the production of the material that builds up. In the case of Tay-Sachs disease, this means reducing the amount of GM2 ganglioside in the body to keep it from building up. The body is deprived of the substrate—hence the name substrate deprivation therapy. One approach to this therapy uses lipid blockers—chemicals that "block" a lipid from being created. This also is called "inhibiting" the production of the substrate. In the case of Tay-Sachs, GM2 ganglioside is the lipid being blocked.

Clinical trials (the testing on people of a drug or therapy that has not yet been approved for general use) have begun utilizing chemicals called *inhibitors* that block the production of GM2 ganglioside. One chemical that is being studied is called N-butyldeoxynojirimycin. This compound has been demonstrated to help in type I Gaucher disease (the most common lipid storage disease). It has also shown promise in treating mice with Sandhoff disease, which is closely related to Tay-Sachs. The mice lived longer and were without symptoms for a longer period of time than untreated mice. It is not yet known whether N-butyldeoxynojirimycin will also help in Tay-Sachs, in which the lipid builds up mostly in the brain.

Currently, clinical trials are being carried out in people with late-onset Tay-Sachs. Substrate deprivation therapy holds particular promise for treating the late-onset forms of the disease because these patients produce a small amount of hex A. If the production rate of GM2 ganglioside could be significantly slowed down, then the amount of hex A enzyme these patients produce might be sufficient to break down the amount of GM2 ganglioside in the body. However, achieving the proper balance is important when applying this type of treatment. Substances such as GM2 ganglioside are important to the proper functioning of nerves and, therefore, cannot be entirely eliminated from the body. For this reason, some researchers are suggesting that a combination of enzyme replacement therapy and substrate deprivation therapy may be more effective than either method used alone.

METABOLIC BYPASS THERAPY

Metabolism describes the processes that take place within the body, such as the creation and breaking down of substances like lipids. An experimental approach called **metabolic bypass therapy** is aimed at discovering whether there are other ways of breaking down GM2 ganglioside to prevent it from building up in the brain. Such a solution would simply bypass the whole metabolic process of the hex A enzyme breaking down the GM2 ganglioside. Therefore, this approach is called metabolic bypass therapy.

To accomplish this, scientists use chemicals to make more of other enzymes that break down GM2 ganglioside or try to make the existing enzymes more active so they are more effective. Experiments have been done in this area using mice. For example, in one experiment, researchers at the Montreal Children's Hospital Research Institute and Department of Human Genetics, at McGill University in Quebec, Canada, have demonstrated that the activity of the enzyme sialidase can be increased to break down GM2 gangliosides to a safe level.

In addition to the approaches discussed in this chapter, researchers are investigating various methods of gene therapy to treat diseases such as Tay-Sachs.

7

GENE-BASED TREATMENTS

*G*enetic engineering is the process of altering genes in order to fix defects that cause diseases. This chapter discusses what researchers have learned about genes, the various techniques that can be used to repair defective genes, and the different ways that scientists are using genetic engineering techniques to try to cure diseases such as Tay-Sachs.

THE HUMAN GENOME PROJECT AND GENETIC DISEASES

One of the most exciting projects that has paved the way for genetic engineering approaches to treating diseases is the Human Genome Project. (A genome is broadly described as the DNA found in all the chromosomes of an organism.) The $3 billion Human Genome Project was started in 1988. Its headquarters was located at the National Institutes of Health, in Bethesda, Maryland, and the work was carried out by geneticists in the United States, France, Japan, China, the United Kingdom, and Germany. Its original goal was to sequence the DNA in human chromosomes to create a complete map of the structure of our DNA. The project was an international effort coordinated by the U.S. Department of

FIGURE 7.1 James Watson, one of the scientists credited with discovering the structure of DNA, volunteered to have his genome sequenced and published online as part of the Human Genome Project.

Energy and National Institutes of Health (NIH). Scientists in the participating countries all contributed their efforts.

James Watson, one of the original discoverers of the structure of DNA, was the first head of the project and directed it until 1992. He was succeeded by Francis Collins, a physician-geneticist, who previously was professor of internal medicine and human genetics at the University of Michigan. He developed a method of crossing large stretches of DNA to identify disease genes, a method he dubbed "positional cloning," which has been successfully used to find the genes responsible for diseases such as cystic fibrosis and Huntington's disease.

The goal was to complete the sequencing of the human genome by 2005. However, by the 1990s, new machines were developed that could sequence genes much faster than the manual methods previously used by researchers. As a result, the work went much faster than expected.

In 1998, the government-run Human Genome Project got some unexpected competition when Dr. J. Craig Venter, along with Applera Corporation of Norwalk, Connecticut, jointly founded Celera Genomics, located in Rockville, Maryland. This new company's goal was to beat the Human Genome Project in sequencing the human genome. Dr. Venter had developed a method for sequencing long strands of DNA, which has come to be known as "shotgun sequencing" or "shotgun cloning." He wanted to prove that his method was superior to the traditional method used in the Human Genome Project. These two factors led to a much faster sequencing of the genome than originally expected.

In 2000, the initial sequencing of the genome was completed, and the results were announced jointly by the Human Genome Project and Celera Genomics in recognition of both teams' efforts. A draft version of the sequence of the human genome was published in 2001. The Human Genome Project was officially concluded in 2003 when the final version of the genome was produced. By identifying the location of every gene and the pattern of bases in it, the Human Genome Project has provided an invaluable tool for research into the diagnosis and treatment of genetic diseases such as Tay-Sachs.

Developing diagnostic and therapeutic treatments and products from information provided by the Human Genome Project, however, requires more than just knowledge of the location of genes and their composition. Researchers must still figure out the function of each gene and how different genes interact with each other. Nonetheless, the project has provided researchers with the ability to identify many genes that are responsible for diseases such as Tay-Sachs.

In addition, the tools and techniques developed during the course of the project have proved valuable to researchers in identifying specific mutations that are associated with such diseases.

WHAT HAVE WE LEARNED FROM THE HUMAN GENOME PROJECT?

The human genome contains approximately 30,000 genes. All humans have almost exactly the same DNA—the sequence of 99.9% of the bases in everyone's DNA is identical. Since the sequencing of the genome, scientists have identified the functions of approximately half the genes discovered.

Only about 2% of the DNA in the genome makes up genes that encode the patterns for proteins. Some stretches of DNA contain combinations of bases that do not code for any protein. Scientists have dubbed these inactive stretches of DNA "nonsense DNA." Approximately half the DNA in the genome is made up of these repeated "nonsense" sequences. Scientists do not know what the purpose of nonsense DNA is, but they think that one of its functions is periodically to make new genes or mix with existing genes to modify them. This is part of the process called evolution. (Evolution allows organisms, including people, to develop new traits that make them better able to survive as their environment changes.)

The locations on the genome that are the most interesting to researchers are the ones where a single base differs among people. These single points of difference are called single-nucleotide polymorphism (*poly* means "many" and *morphism* means "shape(s).") Those are the points that most commonly allow researchers to identify genes responsible for particular diseases. However, there are 1.4 million of these locations, so there is a lot of work to do. Knowing the sequence of the human genome allows scientists to study how multiple genes in one tissue or organ work together to allow that tissue or organ to function properly. It also provides information as to what happens when one of those genes malfunctions.

TYPES OF TAY-SACHS GENETIC MUTATIONS

Over a hundred different mutations have been identified that can cause Tay-Sachs disease. All of these mutations occur in the HEXA gene on chromosome 15, which **encodes** (contains the pattern for) the alpha subunit of the hex A enzyme. This is one of the two subunits that produce the two parts of the enzyme that are required to break down GM2 ganglioside.

Among the mutations that cause Tay-Sachs are:

◆ **Base pair insertions:** As explained in Chapter 1, there are four chemical bases that make up the pattern in a gene that determines what protein that gene produces. The bases are: adenine (A), guanine (G), cytosine (C), and thymine (T). In a base pair insertion, a pair of bases that do not belong in the protein are accidentally added to the part of the gene that encodes for it. This means that the protein will not be produced correctly.

◆ **Base pair deletions:** In this case, a base pair that is necessary to produce the protein correctly is missing from the gene.

◆ **Point mutations:** The insertion or deletion of a single base at a specific location on a gene.

A variety of other, more complicated, mutations is also possible. However, the mutations just described are some of the most common in Tay-Sachs. For example, the most common mutation on the HEXA gene seen in the Ashkenazi Jewish population is a four-base-pair insertion. A different mutation occurs commonly in people of French-Canadian ancestry. In this case a long sequence of bases in the gene is deleted.

WHAT IS GENE THERAPY?

Gene therapy is the use of modern technology to correct diseases caused by the mutation of a gene. Although gene therapy is still in the experimental stage, there are scientists working worldwide to find ways to repair malfunctioning genes. There are several different types of gene therapy:

◆ The replacement of a defective gene with a gene that works correctly.

◆ The repair of a defective gene by removing the defective area and replacing it with a correct segment.

◆ Turning the functioning of a gene on or off by altering other genes that control them. This is useful in genes that cause cancer by addressing the gene that allows cells to grow out of control. In this case turning them off can be beneficial.

The first two types of genetic therapy described next are the types most likely to be beneficial in the treatment of Tay-Sachs disease.

SOMATIC AND GERMLINE GENE THERAPY

The type of gene therapy that accounts for most of the research that is currently taking place is called **somatic gene therapy**. (*Somatic* means "relating to the body.") This type of therapy is aimed at changing the DNA in the cells that make up the tissues and organs in the human body. The other type of gene therapy is called **germline therapy**. This type of therapy is aimed at changing the DNA in sperm and egg cells (also called "germ cells"). The goal here is to change the DNA that is passed on to people's children. Germline therapy is much more controversial than somatic gene therapy because it affects not just the person being treated, but potentially the human race as whole.

All of the body's cells reproduce periodically: Old cells die and are replaced with new ones. Over a person's lifetime, every cell in the body is replaced about 50 times. When cells reproduce, they duplicate their genes. When a defective gene is replaced with a new one, the resulting cell will pass the new DNA on when it reproduces. This is the basis of a lot of gene therapy. Scientists have an opportunity to insert new genes, which are reproduced when the old cells are replaced by the new cells.

HOW DOES GENE THERAPY WORK?

The first thing scientists need to know is the sequence of the DNA that needs to be replaced. This is one area where the information learned from the Human Genome Project is valuable.

The root of gene therapy is based on inserting a working copy of the gene into the cells of a person who lacks a functioning copy of that gene. This is a challenge because the membrane that surrounds the nucleus of the cell is designed to keep most things out to protect chromosomes in the nucleus from damage. One of the few things that can get through the membrane are viruses. Viruses are microscopic balls of DNA surrounded by a protective shell. Viruses reproduce by invading cells and inserting their DNA into the

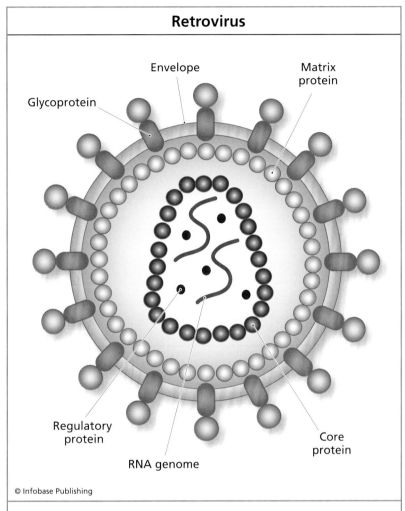

Retrovirus

Glycoprotein

Envelope

Matrix
protein

Regulatory
protein

RNA genome

Core
protein

© Infobase Publishing

FIGURE 7.2 A retrovirus can be used in gene therapy to insert a
new, healthy gene to replace a defective gene.

nucleus. The viruses then take over the cellular "machin-
ery" and use it to churn out more copies of themselves.

Since viruses are already designed to do the work of
inserting DNA into the cell, they make an excellent delivery mechanism to transport new genes. In gene therapy,

of course, it would not make sense to use an active virus that causes a disease to transport the new DNA. Instead, scientists use several specific types of viruses. In all cases, scientists remove the viruses' own DNA and replace it with the segment they want to insert into the cell. The most common types of viruses used in gene therapy are:

- *Retroviruses*: *Retro* means "reverse." Retroviruses contain a single strand of **ribonucleic acid (RNA)**. This RNA consists of a sequence of bases that provide the pattern, or template, to create a particular segment of DNA. The retrovirus delivers this RNA into the cell's nucleus. The cell then uses it to make new DNA, which is incorporated into the cell's DNA. This allows the retrovirus to use the cell's DNA copying capability to copy itself. Therapeutically, this allows scientists to insert a new gene in place of an old one.
- *Adenoviruses*: Adenoviruses carry a double strand of DNA. Adenoviruses are responsible for common eye infections and the common cold. They can be used to deliver genes to the cell's nucleus.
- *Herpes simplex virus*: This virus, which is responsible for cold sores, carries a single strand of DNA. The herpes simplex virus infects neurons, which may be useful when trying to perform genetic therapy on brain cells.

Gene therapy works by inserting a gene that functions correctly into a virus. The deactivated viruses are **infused** (inserted in a liquid) into the patient's blood. The viruses enter the cell and insert the new gene into the cell's DNA. When the cell reproduces, the new cells contain the inserted DNA. The

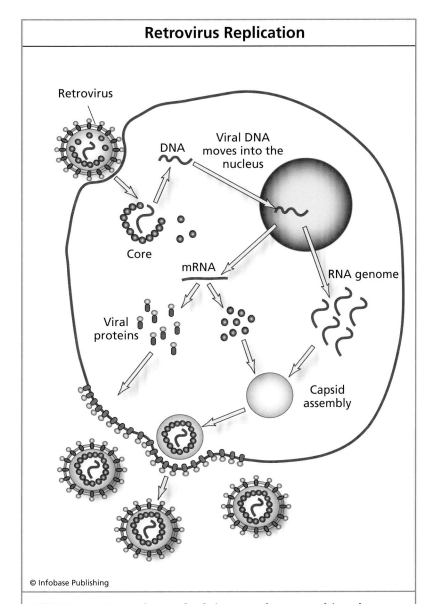

Retrovirus Replication

Retrovirus

DNA

Viral DNA
moves into the
nucleus

Core

mRNA

RNA genome

Viral
proteins

Capsid
assembly

FIGURE 7.3 Retroviruses, both in gene therapy and in other
infections, use the cells they invade to create the components of
new retroviruses.

new, correctly functioning DNA now produces the correctly functioning protein. In the case of Tay-Sachs, this would be the hex A enzyme. The enzyme thus produced would function normally and break down the GM2 ganglioside.

The most common method of getting the virus with the new DNA into a patient's cells is to infuse it into the patient's blood by using an *intravenous system*. This intravenous setup consists of a plastic bag that contains a virus solution which is dripped into the patient's bloodstream through a needle that has been inserted into one of the patient's blood vessels.

NONVIRAL APPROACHES

Even though the viruses used in gene therapy are deactivated, some people are concerned that they could still spread illnesses from one person to another; or, they might still be somewhat active and make the recipient of the virus sick; or, the viruses might be recognized as foreign by the immune system and cause a severe allergic reaction.

Therefore, scientists are also experimenting with nonviral approaches to delivering DNA. This section looks at some of these methods.

Artificial Liposomes

One approach uses an **artificial liposome**, a lipid sphere that has a hollow core. The center of the sphere is filled with fluid containing the DNA that is to be introduced into the cell. Because this fluid is a lipid, it can pass through the cell's membrane and deliver the DNA. In 2003, William Pardridge and colleagues at the University of California, Los Angeles, successfully used artificial liposomes to transport a protein called *luciferase*, which glows, into the brains of primates to prove that this technique could be used to carry molecules across the blood-brain barrier. They subsequently used the artificial liposomes to carry a gene across the blood-brain barrier in rats to treat Parkinson's disease, a disease that destroys the brain cells that produce the chemical dopamine and causes a person's muscles to become rigid and paralyzed. This type of technology may someday prove useful for treating not only Parkinson's but also other neurological diseases.

Artificial Chromosomes

Another approach that is being investigated is the creation of an **artificial chromosome**. The goal is to introduce this chromosome into the cell, where it will be reproduced along with the other chromosomes in the cell during cell reproduction. The advantage of this approach is that it can deliver a large amount of DNA, perhaps even enough to tackle multiple problems. The challenge lies in successfully inserting such a large object into the cell.

Many molecules pass through the cell membrane by attaching (binding) to a receptor on the outside of the membrane. (A receptor is an element that "receives" something.) The receptor acts like a lock. When a molecule with an appropriate shape fits into it, this causes pores in the membrane to open and allow the molecule to pass through. Some researchers have attempted to attach DNA to one of the "key" molecules as a way of getting the DNA into the cell. So far, however, this method has had less success than other approaches.

POTENTIAL OF GENE THERAPY TO TREAT TAY-SACHS

Even if a gene replacement therapy for Tay-Sachs disease is successfully developed, the time frame for when it can be most effectively applied will present challenges. One of the problems is that once the nerve cells in the brain have been damaged from the buildup of lipid, a child's functioning may be permanently affected. However, children's brains are more pliable than adults', so it is possible that they will recover their function better than adults would. It also may someday be possible to combine gene replacement therapy with another therapy that replaces neurons, such as stem cell implants, or the use of chemicals such as neuronal growth factor to make new connections. (Neuronal growth factor is a chemical produced in the body that causes neurons to sprout branchlike structures called *dendrites* that are used to connect to other neurons.)

Researchers will not know how much brain function can be recovered until gene therapy reaches the point where it can be applied to human beings. Therefore, it is likely that once such a therapy becomes usable, it will work best if used along with newborn screening procedures to identify children who have a defective gene for the hex A enzyme before it has a chance to do damage. Since the first symptoms of Tay-Sachs do not become apparent until the child is several months old, it is important that a newborn screening procedure that identifies Tay-Sachs be used so that it can be treated immediately, before significant damage is done.

ISSUES OF GENETIC ENGINEERING APPROACHES

There are a number of obstacles that need to be overcome before gene therapy can be used successfully. A basic problem is the short-term nature of current approaches to gene therapy. It is not enough to introduce new DNA into the patient's cells. It must be incorporated into the patient's chromosomes so that when the cells reproduce, the new DNA continues to be copied as well. Otherwise, as their cells keep dividing and producing new cells, patients must undergo repeated treatments to add new functioning DNA.

Another issue is that the delivery method for the DNA can, in some cases, cause a severe immune system reaction. This happens because the body senses the DNA as being a foreign particle, which causes it to attack what it sees as an invading organism. When the "foreign agent" enters cells throughout the human body, so many of those cells may find themselves under attack by immune system cells that it could lead to organ damage and possibly result in death. There is also a danger that new genes could interact in unexpected ways with other genes to cause cancer or unanticipated health problems.

There are other issues related to the use of viruses as a delivery method, such as the infection of someone with a disease or the accidental spread of the virus with the new DNA to other people. Another concern is that the viruses with the new DNA might be incorporated into the sperm or egg cells of affected people who are the right age to reproduce. What effect the foreign DNA will have on their children is unknown. Experiments with mice have shown that it is possible to infuse new genes into fertilized cells and produce offspring with the new gene. However, the offspring had problems with growth and **fertility** (the ability to produce babies). While it may be possible to work out the problems eventually, germ-line therapy is an area where great care needs to be taken.

Other issues that remain to be addressed include practical ones. Gene therapy is labor-intensive and it involves a great deal of time and effort to produce a small amount of DNA. Because of this, the therapy is very expensive and likely to remain so for a long time. Many health insurance companies have traditionally declined to pay for experimental treatments, even ones that have been around for a long time, such as bone marrow transplants.

ADVANTAGES OF GENE THERAPY

The obvious advantage of gene therapy is that it could provide a way to treat diseases that are currently untreatable. If successful, germline therapy techniques could be developed, and it might be possible to alter the DNA of sperm and egg cells through gene therapy. This approach could have the potential to replace defective genes for Tay-Sachs and other genetic disorders so that they are simply not present when a baby is born.

The discovery of treatments for genetic disorders could lead to an increased early detection of people with disease-causing defective genes and, therefore, lead to early

OVERSEEING GENE THERAPY

In the United States, the Food and Drug Administration (FDA) is responsible for ensuring the safety of medications and medical devices. It is also responsible for overseeing clinical trials of new therapeutic treatments such as gene therapy. The Center for Biologics Evaluation and Research (CBER) is the FDA branch that is responsible for overseeing gene therapy. The FDA approves clinical trials and provides guidelines for researchers on how to conduct them. This includes follow-ups to monitor the status of patients after they have been treated. In addition, a team of experts from the FDA travels to the manufacturer's testing and research sites to make sure the companies and research labs are following the regulations provided by the FDA.

The FDA has a special committee that reviews issues related to gene therapy. It is called the Biological Response Modifiers Advisory Committee (BRMAC). The FDA works closely with the U.S. National Institutes of Health (NIH). The NIH is responsible intervention. Currently, though, there is a reluctance to test young people for genetic defects, even though the tests are available. People who find they have a gene that may lead to a disabling and untreatable disease may simply become overwhelmed with worry. For diseases that cannot yet be treated, there is no benefit to doing this. On the other hand, there would be no reason not to test children for diseases that could be treated. Diseases such as Tay-Sachs could be detected early through approaches such as newborn testing. In addition, the tests would alleviate worry of families of those children who are at risk but have been found not to have the defective gene.

for promoting research into new technologies that can improve people's health. Among other things, they provide funding for promising technologies. The NIH also funds research projects to develop new and better techniques for gene therapy. It also provides funding for many clinical trials in gene therapy. In contrast, the FDA is responsible for ensuring that gene products and therapies are safe and effective, as well as supervising the implementation of clinical trials.

In 2004, the FDA and NIH jointly developed a database on human gene transfer information that can be accessed by computer over the Internet. Called the Genetic Modification Clinical Research Information System (GeMCRIS), it provides a more effective way for researchers to report and analyze problems that arise in gene therapy clinical trials. In addition, it provides information on gene therapy directly to the public. The public part of the database can be accessed at www.gemcris.od.nih.gov.

CLINICAL TRIALS

Gene therapy is still in a very experimental stage and is currently not available to the general public. However, a number of clinical trials are currently being conducted.

Before a therapy can be tested in people, it must first be tested in animals. A variety of other procedures will follow to make sure that the therapy is effective and has minimal side effects. Any substance used to treat people, including one used in gene therapy, must be combined with other compounds to see how it will react with them; for example, researchers will combine it with cells that produce the compound it is supposed to break down to see if it works, and then give various doses to animals such as rats. It is much more difficult to ensure the safety of gene therapy at this point than it is with standard medications. There is still a great deal researchers do not know about how the human body will react to the introduction of foreign DNA.

Clinical trials are conducted under controlled conditions in a series of phases or steps. This approach also allows researchers or the government agencies overseeing the trials to stop the trial if it appears to be too dangerous to the patients.

Participating in a Clinical Trial

There are many risks associated with an experimental treatment. The treatment may have unexpected side effects and the body may also react to it in a negative way. So, why do people accept the risk and agree to participate? Sometimes people whose children have an untreatable disease like Tay-Sachs feel that even the slightest hope that the treatment will make them suffer less or live longer makes it worth the risk. This is especially true of diseases that affect children. However, there is also another reason for participating in studies. Many of those who know that there is no treatment or cure for their problem today believe that by taking part in these studies, they will be making a lasting contribution to solving a problem that will improve the lives of other people in the future and hopefully lead to a cure.

Every study advances the medical community's knowledge of how to treat a disease. This is even true of those experiments that are not successful. They can be very valuable in telling researchers what approaches do not work and help pinpoint specific problems that still must be addressed. Sometimes, clarifying a problem allows scientists to develop a means to address it in the future. A treatment that does show some benefit assures scientists that they are moving in the right direction so they can continue to improve the process.

COPING WITH
TAY-SACHS

This chapter explores some of the issues faced by people
who have a child or **sibling** (a brother or sister) with Tay-
Sachs disease.

TREATMENT

Since there is no cure for Tay-Sachs, all treatments for the
disease are aimed at easing the suffering of patients. The
goal is to reduce the symptoms as much as possible and
keep the child comfortable. For example, doctors prescribe
medications that control muscle spasms and seizures. Since
the type and severity of seizures can change over time,
monitoring the effectiveness of the medication and making
necessary changes to it as needed are crucial.

COPING WITH HEALTH PROBLEMS

Children who are severely disabled with Tay-Sachs disease
require a great deal of specialized medical care. Children
may have issues with their eyes, nose, and lungs as well as
muscle-related problems. They may have trouble swallowing
and experience difficulty breathing because of the mucus that
clogs up the nose or lungs. They may develop **asthma** (spasms

in the airways in the lungs) and **pneumonia** (a bacterial infection of the lungs). To help minimize these problems, children are often moved into different positions such as sitting or lying down, or lying on their side. Managing these problems becomes more critical as the disease progresses. Children may be confined to a wheelchair and later to a bed. Eventually, they may not be able to move at all. Children may also require special medical devices that remove mucus or help with breathing. Initially, children with Tay-Sachs can be spoon-fed like other children. However, as swallowing difficulties develop, it may be necessary to use a special feeding tube.

Children with Tay-Sachs often have trouble sleeping at night because of the discomfort caused by muscle spasms

FIGURE 8.1 Matthew and Mary Cairns play with their sons Isaiah, 11 months, and Ethan, 2. Isaiah was diagnosed with Tay-Sachs disease the month before, and his quality of life is expected to seriously diminish by age 2.

or difficulty with breathing. This can make it impossible for parents and siblings to get the rest they need. Sleeping medication can help a child sleep through the night.

PLAYING

Children with neurological disorders like Tay-Sachs still enjoy playing as much as healthy kids do. For an older child to play with a sick or disabled child is important and rewarding. Children with Tay-Sachs frequently have trouble moving around, so play that engages their senses is good. Musical toys, mobiles, and puppets encourage children to use their senses, including the sense of sight, even if it is affected. Play does more than help a child exercise sight and hearing, however. It also provides human interaction. Toys that are large, bright, and shiny are generally good because they provide a lot of sensory input and are easier for a child with coordination problems to handle than small toys. Care should be taken, of course, to make sure they are "baby-safe" with no small, sharp, or hard components. If a sibling is playing with a child who has Tay-Sachs, it is important to remember that these children are very sensitive and toys that make loud or sudden sharp noises may not be a good choice.

Siblings might be hesitant or afraid of touching or holding their brother or sister because they know the child is sick and are afraid of hurting them. In reality, all children need to be touched and held. Patting, hugging, and other gentle contact is important to any child's comfort and security, especially for a child with a chronic illness. While it is not a good idea to play rough with an ill sibling, gentler forms of play are perfectly fine and helpful in building a relationship. If there are special problems involved in handling a sibling as the disease progresses, parents and medical professionals are available to provide guidance as to an appropriate degree of contact. It is important to understand that Tay-Sachs is a genetic disease and is not *contagious* (capable of spreading from one person to another).

FAMILY RELATIONSHIPS

Having a child with a neurological disorder such as Tay-Sachs can put a great deal of strain on family relationships. Caring for a sick child is extremely time consuming and a tremendous amount of work. The fact that the child requires so much attention means that other members of the family may receive less. Dealing with a disabled child can sometimes bring a couple closer together as they work to cope with the problem. In other cases, it can put a serious strain on their relationship. This is true because, as mentioned in the National Tay-Sachs and Allied Diseases Association (NTSAD) Web site, people may feel anger at having a child with Tay-Sachs and may take it out on whoever is around; this often turns out to be other family members.

According to an article titled "When a Sibling Is Disabled," by Dr. Lawrence Kutner, parents need to ensure that other children in the family do not feel neglected or left out because a sick sibling appears to be getting all the attention. Getting siblings involved in caring for the sick child can make everyone feel a part of what is happening in the family. However, siblings may feel that sometimes their parents put too much of a burden on them. At other times, parents may be reluctant to let a sibling help because they feel they are putting an unfair burden on the sibling. Parents do not always understand that it is better for a sibling to be included in dealing with a family problem than to be ignored. It is not easy having a brother or sister who has Tay-Sachs disease. It is very painful to watch someone you love decline and pass away. Having a sibling with a disease like Tay-Sachs may mean that parents have less time and attention to devote to other children in the family. This may make the other children feel ignored or lonely. The demands of providing supportive treatment and medication for a brother or sister may also mean that parents have less money to spend on other things, which may make other family members feel resentful. At the same time, it is natural to feel guilty about having occasional feelings of resentment or anger toward a brother or sister who is sick.

Siblings may also worry that they may give birth to a child with the disease someday. They need to keep in mind that there are simple screening tests to find out if they are a carrier of a gene for Tay-Sachs. A number of advances in medicine make it possible to have children even if both partners are carriers. As the years go by, it is likely that advances will continue to be made in both reproductive technology and treatments for Tay-Sachs.

RESPITE CARE

Respite care is short-term care that is provided through various organizations, including hospices, and home health personal care services. Volunteer home help services are provided through churches, synagogues, and other faith-based organizations. They allow family members to take a break from caring for a sick child. This type of break can give other family members a chance to interact with each other in a less stressful way.

Respite care is provided for periods ranging from a few days to several weeks. Information on providers of respite care can be obtained through local hospitals or medical centers, state departments of both health and child services, local support organizations for disabled children, local **hospices** (facilities that provide supportive care to those who are dying), and the ARCH National Respite Care Network, which maintains a directory of respite care providers on its Web site (www.archrespite.org).

LIVING WITH LATE-ONSET TAY-SACHS

The effects of late-onset Tay-Sachs differ significantly from person to person. People with late-onset Tay-Sachs often live with family members or in their own home. In the latter case, they may require assistance from paid home health aids or visiting nurses, and special services such as Meals on Wheels (which delivers meals to the elderly and disabled). State departments of social services can assist with information on special services and funding for assistance. The U.S. Department of Health and Human Services can also provide this information.

People with late-onset Tay-Sachs disease often continue to work at their profession for a significant period of time. The Americans with Disabilities Act of 1990 protects people with disabilities from job discrimination. If the disease causes difficulties, this act requires your employer to make reasonable changes so that you are able to continue working. These changes can include changing your duties or allowing you to work part-time. It also might include providing special equipment or devices, such as installing a wheelchair ramp or a computer monitor that will magnify the type to a very large size.

Those with a disabling disease such as Tay-Sachs that have been working but have to quit their jobs may be eligible to receive disability payments from the U.S. Social Security Administration and may also receive Supplemental Income Assistance payments from the same source. A person who is disabled may also be eligible to receive Medicare or Medicaid coverage to pay for medical treatment. The Social

Security Administration can also provide information on these programs.

Those with late-onset Tay-Sachs may need medication to cope with a variety of physical symptoms, including muscle spasms and tremors (trembling or shaking). Difficulties with muscle coordination can make it hard for people with late-onset Tay-Sachs to speak clearly. Some of the techniques that can be used to improve communication are speaking more slowly and exaggerating the sounds of letters in words. An expert in speech-language disorders, called a **speech-language pathologist**, can often help to develop techniques to allow a person with late-onset Tay-Sachs to communicate better. Speech-language therapists evaluate speech difficulties and provide help in speaking more clearly. They can also assist people with obtaining and using alternative communication devices, ranging from word/picture boards to electronic devices that "speak" for a person. **Physical therapists** provide exercise therapies that help with muscle-related problems such as coordination, spasms, and weakness, and **occupational therapists** can train a person in different ways of doing daily tasks such as dressing, bathing, and eating. These therapists can help people obtain special utensils that make doing these tasks easier. Examples of such devices include a stick with a loop on the end that pulls buttons through buttonholes; flatware with a handle that slips over a person's hand to make manipulating forks, knives, and spoons easier; and plastic stools, handrails, and shower heads that are attached to a flexible cable to make showering easier.

Patients with late-onset Tay-Sachs may suffer from psychological problems such as depression or hallucinations. *Antidepressant* or **antipsychotic** medications may be given. Because the psychological problems are the result of physical changes in the brain, such medications are not always effective. Even if psychological symptoms are not produced by the disease itself, coping with any chronic medical problem and the resulting discomfort can cause problems such as depression. In addition to taking medication, many people find it beneficial to talk with a psychiatrist or counselor. There are support groups available in most areas for those suffering from late-onset Tay-Sachs. In addition, there are organizations that offer online forums for discussing issues related to living with late-onset Tay-Sachs disease. Medical facilities, community groups, and the Internet are sources of information on such groups. Many people with late-onset Tay-Sachs live a normal life span (currently estimated at the mid-seventies in the United States), so it is important to take advantage of the available services and support to make their lives as comfortable as possible.

GLOSSARY

Abortion   The removal of the fetus from the womb to end a pregnancy.

Activator protein   A protein that works with an enzyme to cause a chemical reaction to occur.

Acute   A medical term applied to diseases whose symptoms are short and severe.

Allele   A specific form of a gene for a particular trait (such as the version that produces blue eye color or brown eye color).

Amino acids   Molecules made up of various combinations of the elements hydrogen, carbon, oxygen, and nitrogen. Proteins are made of amino acids.

Antibody   A Y-shaped protein that attaches to foreign particles in the blood.

Antipsychotic   Medication used to treat a number of serious psychological disorders, such as paranoia, which could cause people to accidentally hurt themselves or someone else.

Aramaic   An ancient language spoken in Syria, Palestine, and Mesopotamia.

Artificial chromosome   A chromosome produced in a laboratory and inserted into a patient to provide new DNA.

Artificial liposome   A hollow ball of fat created in a laboratory and used to deliver new DNA to a patient.

Ashkenazi   Jews of Eastern European ancestry.

Asthma   A condition in which a person experiences spasms in the airways that make it difficult to breath.

Biochemistry   The study of how chemicals are produced and work in the body.

Blastocyst   A mass of cells produced from a fertilized egg.

Blood-brain barrier   A layer of cells in the brain's blood vessels that filters out harmful substances.

Bone marrow transplantation   The replacement of a person's unhealthy bone marrow cells with healthy cells from a donor.

Brain stem reflexes   Responses initiating in the area at the base of the brain, which controls involuntary functions such as breathing.

Cancer   Cells of a given type that grow out of control.

Carrier   A person who does not have a disease, but possesses a gene for it.

Cerebral cortex   The part of the brain responsible for high-level mental functions such as learning and reasoning.

Cerebrospinal fluid   Fluid that flows through the brain and spinal cord.

Chemotherapy   The use of strong chemicals to kill fast-growing cancer cells.

Chorionic villus sampling   A type of prenatal testing in which a sample is taken from the placenta.

Chromosomes   Hair-like structures composed of DNA that carry our genetic information.

Clinical trial   The testing of a therapy in human beings that has not yet been approved for general use, but that has previously undergone preliminary testing.

Dementia   Mental confusion.

Deoxyribonucleic acid (DNA) The genetic material that carries the genetic code that produces all the proteins in the human body.

Depression Excessive sadness and gloom.

Dominant gene A gene that will produce a trait if only one copy of that gene is present.

Embryo The cluster of fertilized egg cells that will develop into a fetus.

Embryonic stem cell replacement therapy A process in which fertilized egg cells are grown in a lab or taken from a discarded embryo and transplanted into a person where they will grow into healthy cells of the same type of tissue into which they are implanted.

Encoded Containing the pattern for making a particular gene.

Enzyme A substance produced by the human body that controls a chemical process in the body.

Epidemic The spreading of a disease to a large number of people.

Eugenics The selective mating of individuals to produce offspring with specific genetic traits.

Fertility The ability to reproduce.

Fetus A baby that is developing in the womb.

Founder effect The creation of a new population by a small number of people who carry only a small portion of the gene pool.

Ganglion A type of nerve cell located somewhere other than the brain and spinal cord.

Ganglioside A type of fat found in nerve cells called ganglions.

Gene pool The variety of different genes that are available to be passed on from generation to generation.

Gene therapy   The use of modern technology to fix diseases caused by genetic mutations.

Genetic disease   An ailment that children inherit from their parents.

Genetic disorder   When a genetic mutation causes a protein to function incorrectly or not to be made at all, affecting the health or development of the body.

Genetic drift   The tendency of a trait to become more or less prevalent as it moves through generations.

Genetic engineering   The process of changing genes to fix defects.

Geneticist   An expert in diseases caused by defective genes.

Germline mutation   A change in a gene that takes place in a sperm or egg cell.

Germline therapy   The attempt to cure diseases by changing the DNA in sperm and egg cells so that future generations will be healthy.

Hallucinations   Seeing or hearing things that are not there.

Haploid   A Greek word for single cells.

Hereditary disease   A disease passed from parent to child.

Hippocampus   A seahorse-shaped structure in the middle of the brain that processes memories.

Hospice   A facility that provides supportive care to the dying.

Human Genome Project   An international project that identified the location of every gene and the pattern of bases in it. It has provided an invaluable tool for research into the diagnosis and treatment of genetic diseases.

Hydrolysis   A chemical reaction in which water is used to dissolve a compound.

Immune system   The organs and cells that protect the body from disease.

Immunoassay   A test that uses components of the immune system to identify the presence of a disease.

Inbreeding   Mating between closely related members of a population.

Infuse   To drip a solution into a patient's bloodstream.

Intravenous   Inserted into a vein.

In vitro fertilization   The process of fertilizing an egg cell outside of the body.

Late-onset Tay-Sachs   A form of Tay-Sachs that occurs in adults rather than children.

Lipid   A fatty substance produced in the body.

Lipid storage disorder   Failure to produce lipid results in this type of disease that damages body cells and tissues.

Lysosomal storage disease   A disease that results from a problem in breaking down fat in cells.

Lysosomes   Tiny organ-like structures responsible for digesting, or breaking down, substances in the cell that are no longer necessary.

Meiosis   Cell division wherein the 23 pairs of chromosomes are still duplicated, but division takes place twice.

Metabolic bypass therapy   A method of eliminating a harmful material in the body without relying on the body's natural process for eliminating it.

Metabolic disease   A disease caused by the malfunctioning of processes in the body.

Metabolism   The combination of all the processes that take place in the body.

Mitochondria   Tiny organ-like structures in cells that break down food.

Mitochondrial DNA   DNA found in mitochondria.

Mitosis   Cell division wherein all the contents of an existing, or parent, cell are duplicated, including all of the 46 chromosomes in the nucleus.

Motor skills   Skills requiring muscle control, such as walking.

Myelin   A fatty material that supports and insulates nerve cells.

Neurological   Related to the nerves or the brain.

Neurologist   A doctor who specializes in diseases of the brain and nerves.

Neurons   Nerve cells in the brain.

Occupational therapist   A medical professional who helps people with disabilities with work and living issues.

Ophthalmologist   A doctor who specializes in eye diseases.

Ophthalmoscope   An instrument through which a doctor can view the back of the eye.

Paranoia   Unreasonable fear.

Parkinson's disease   A disease that destroys the brain cells that produce the chemical dopamine and leads to the inability to use the muscles.

Paternal   On the father's side.

Physical therapist   A medical professional who provides therapy for muscle- and disability-related problems.

Placenta   The organ in the womb that attaches the fetus to the mother's blood supply, providing nourishment and eliminating waste products.

Plasmid   A ring of DNA that occurs in bacteria and yeast and is used to create recombinant DNA.

Pneumonia   An infection of the lungs.

Polymerase chain reaction A technique for multiplying strands of DNA in order to make quantities large enough to analyze.

Population bottleneck A subset of genetic traits from a parent population that becomes common in a particular subpopulation.

Predominate To be stronger than other factors.

Pre-implantation testing Testing in vitro fertilized embryos for defects before placing them in the womb.

Prenatal Before birth.

Psychological Relating to the functioning of the mind.

Radioactive Giving off rays of energy.

Recessive gene A gene that will only produce a trait if a person inherits two copies of the gene.

Recombinant DNA DNA created by combined DNA from two sources.

Reflex An involuntary action.

Respite care Short-term care for a sick person, designed to give family members a break from caring for the sick person.

Retina The reflective layer of cells at the back of the eyeball.

Ribonucleic acid (RNA) A substance made up of a sequence that corresponds to a complementary strand of DNA. It is used in the process of making DNA.

Seizure Sudden uncontrollable muscle spasms.

Sialic acid A building block of glycoproteins like GM2 ganglioside.

Sibling A brother or sister.

Somatic cell A body cell, rather than a sperm or egg cell.

Somatic gene therapy The attempt to cure a disease by changing the DNA in the cells that make up the tissues in a person's body.

Speech-language pathologist An expert in speech and language disorders.

Spinal cord The bundle of nerves running down the back that carries signals to and from the brain.

Spontaneous mutation A random change in a gene that occurs when chromosomes are being copied.

Starch-gel electrophoresis A method for separating and measuring the amount of various molecules present in a person's blood and cells.

Stem cell An immature cell produced in the bone marrow that can develop into many different types of cells.

Subacute A medical term applied to diseases that are moderate in length and seriousness.

Subpopulation A small group within a larger a population in which all members of the group have certain common characteristics.

Substrate A substance acted on by an enzyme.

Substrate deprivation therapy A method of keeping a disease-causing material from being produced in the body.

Synthesis The process by which a protein is assembled from various elements.

Therapeutic cloning The creation of identical cells in a laboratory for treating diseases.

Trait A characteristic.

Tuberculosis A highly contagious lung disease.

Yiddish The common language of Ashkenazi Jews.

BIBLIOGRAPHY

Ananthaswamy, Anil. "Undercover Genes Slip Into the Brain." New Scientist Web site (March 20, 2003). Available online. URL: http://www.newscientist.com/article.ns?id=dn3520. Accessed April 14, 2007.

Behar, Doron M. et al. "The Matrilineal Ancestry of Ashkenazi Jewry: Portrait of a Recent Founder Event." *American Journal of Human Genetics.* American Society of Human Genetics Web site. Available online. URL: http://www.ftdna.com/pdf/43026_Doron.pdf. Accessed November 12, 2006.

Duke University. "Infants With Rare Genetic Disorders Saved by Umbilical Cord Blood Stem Cell Implants." Duke University press release (May 18, 2005). Available online. URL: http://www.dukemednews.org/news/article.php?id=8747. Accessed April 4, 2007.

Fackelmann, Kathy A. "Test-tube Diagnosis: Analyzing Embryos for Genetic Flaws." *Science News* 146.18 (October 28, 1994): 286–287.

Frey, Lauren C., Steven P. Ringel, and Christopher M. Filley. "The Natural History of Cognitive Dysfunction in Late-Onset GM_2 Gangliosidosis." *Archives of Neurology* 62 (2005): 989–994.

Hammer, M F. et al. "Jewish and Middle Eastern Non-Jewish Populations Share a Common Pool of Y-chromosome Biallelic Haplotypes." *Proceedings of the National Academy of Sciences* (May 9, 2000). Available online. URL: http://www.pnas.org/cgi/reprint/97/12/6769.pdf. Accessed April 14, 2007.

Harris, Rodney. "Medical Genetics." *British Medical Journal* 303 (October 19, 1991): 977–999.

Mehler, Mark F. and John A. Kessler. "Progenitor Cell Biology: Implications for Neural Regeneration." *Archives of Neurology* 56 (1999): 780–784.

Meikle, Peter J. et al. "Newborn Screening for Lysosomal Storage Disorders: Clinical Evaluation of a Two-tier Strategy." *Pediatrics* 114.4 (October 2004): 909–916.

National Human Genome Research Institute. "Tay-Sachs." Available online. URL: http://www.genome.gov/page.cfm?pageID=10001220. Accessed January 7, 2007.

National Institute of Neurological Disorders and Stroke. "Lipid Storage Diseases Fact Sheet." NINDS Web site. Available online. URL: http://www.ninds.nih.gov/disorders/lipid_storage_diseases/lipid_storage_diseases.htm.

National Institutes of Health. "Tay Sachs Disease." John Hopkins University Online Mendelian Inheritance in Man Web site. Available online. URL: http://www.ncbi.nlm.nih.gov/entrez/dispomim.cgi?id=272800. Accessed November 12, 2006.

National Tay-Sachs and Allied Disease Association. "Living With LOTS." NTSAD Web site. Available online. URL: http://ntsad.org. Accessed April 14, 2007.

Ohno, Kazuki, Seiji Saito, Kanako Sugawara, and Hitoshi Sakuraba. "Structural Consequences of Amino Acid Substitutions Causing Tay-Sachs Disease." *Molecular Genetics and Metabolism* 94.4 (August 2008): 462–468.

Porter, Rebecca. "New Law Will Protect Employees and Insureds from Genetic Bias." *Trial* 44.7 (July 2008), 70–71.

Quest Diagnostics. "Ashkenazi Jewish Panel." Quest Diagnostics Web site. Available online. URL: http://www.questdiagnostics.com/hcp/topics/ashkenazi/ashkenazi.html. Accessed January 7, 2007.

Risch, Neil, Hua Tang, Howard Katzenstein, and Josef Ekstein. "Geographic Distribution of Disease Mutations in the

Ashkenazi Jewish Population Supports Genetic Drift Over Selection." *American Journal of Human Genetics* 72.4 (April 2003): 812–822.

Triggs-Raine, B.L. et al. "Screening for Carriers of Tay-Sachs Disease Among Ashkenazi Jews. A Comparison of DNA-based and Enzyme-based Tests." *New England Journal of Medicine* 323 (July 5, 1990): 6–12.

Tsuji, Daisuke et al. "Therapeutic Evaluation of GM2 Gangliosides by ELISA Using Anti-GM2 Ganglioside Antibodies." *Clinica Chimica Acta* 378.1–2 (March 2007): 38–41.

University of Michigan DNA Sequencing Core. "How Do We Sequence DNA?" Available online. URL: http://seqcore. brcf.med.umich.edu/doc/educ/dnapr/sequencing.html. Accessed April 20, 2007.

U.S. Department of Engergy. Human Genome Project Web site. Availableonline.URL:http://www.ornl.gov/scitechresources/ Human_Genome/project/info.shtml. Accessed November 12, 2006.

U.S. Food and Drug Administration. "Human Gene Therapy and the Role of the FDA." Available online. URL: http://www.fda. gov/cber/infosheets/genezn.htm. Accessed November 12, 2006.

Wenger, David A., Stephanie Coppola, and Shu-Ling Liu. "Insights Into the Diagnosis and Treatment of Lysosomal Storage Diseases." *Archives of Neurology* 60 (2003): 322–328.

Westphal, Sylvia Pagan. "DNA Nanoballs Boost Gene Therapy." New Scientist.com Web site. URL: http://www.newscientist. com/article.ns?id=dn2257. Accessed April 14, 2007.

FURTHER READING

Boon, Kevin A. *The Human Genome Project: What Does Decoding Mean for Us?* Berkeley Heights, N.J.: Enslow, 2002.

Canini, Mikko. *Genetic Engineering.* Farmington Hills, MI: Greenhaven Press, 2005.

Freedman, Jeri. *America Debates: Stem Cell Research.* New York: Rosen Publishing, 2007.

———. *How Do We Know About Genetics and Heredity.* New York: Rosen Publishing, 2004.

Parker, Steve. *Genetic Engineering.* Chicago: Raintree Press, 2005.

Robinson, Tara Rodden. *Genetics for Dummies.* New York: Wiley & Co., 2005.

Shawker, Thomas H. *Unlocking Your Genetic History: A Step-by-step Guide to Unlocking Your Family's Medical and Genetic History.* Nashville: Thomas Nelson, 2004.

Torr, James D. *Genetic Engineering.* Farmington Hills, MI: Greenhaven Press, 2006.

Walker, Julie. *Tay-Sachs Disease.* New York: Rosen Publishing, 2006.

WEB SITES

American Society of Gene Therapy
www.asgt.org.
This site contains articles with the latest information on gene therapy activities.

Chicago Center for Jewish Genetic Disorders

www.jewishgeneticscenter.org.

This site provides information on genetic disorders that affect Jews.

DNA From the Beginning

http://www.dnaftb.org/dnaftb.

A primer on DNA and genetics.

GeMCRIS

www.gemcris.od.nih.gov.

The public site of the joint Food & Drug Administration/National Institutes of Health database of gene therapy trial information.

Genome News Network

www.genomenewsnetwork.org.

This site provides the latest news on genetic topics.

Kids Genetics

SmithKline Glaxo

www.genetics.gsk.com/kids/index_kids.htm.

A site run by a major pharmaceutical company that explains genetics to young people.

Kid's Health

Gene Therapy and Kids

http://kidshealth.org/parent/system/medical/gene_therapy. html.

An introduction to gene therapy for young people.

Mount Sinai Center for Jewish Genetics

http://www.mssm.edu/jewish_genetics.

Source of information on genetic diseases that affect Jews.

National Tay-Sachs and Allied Diseases Association, Inc.
www.ntsad.org.
Excellent source of general and support information for Tay-Sachs disease.

PICTURE CREDITS

INDEX

ABOUT THE AUTHOR

Jeri Freedman has a B.A. from Harvard University and spent 15 years working in companies in the biomedical and high technology fields. She is the author of more than two dozen other nonfiction young adult books as well as several plays and, under the name Ellen Foxxe, is the coauthor of two science fiction novels. She lives in Boston, Massachusetts.